Master seafarers
the Phoenicians and the Greeks

Published by Periplus Publishing London Ltd
Publisher: Danièle Juncqua-Naveau
Series consultant: Étienne Bernand, professeur honoraire des Universités
Editorial team: Nick Easterbrook, Christopher More, Rebecca Penfold
Production: Sophie Chéry
Research: Jane Lowry
Authors: Muriel Moity, Murielle Rudel, Alain-Xavier Wurst
Reprographics: Periplus Publishing London Ltd
English translation: Atlas Translations Ltd, 14a Goodwin's Court, London WC2N 4LL, UK
© 2003 Periplus Publishing London Ltd, 98 Church Rd, London SW13 0DQ, UK
Printed and bound in Italy by Graphicom

All rights reserved. No part of this publication may be reproduced, stored in a retrieval system, or transmitted in any form or by any means, electronic, mechanical, photocopying, recording or otherwise, without the prior permission of the copyright owner.
ISBN: 1-902699-53-X

Master seafarers

the Phoenicians and the Greeks

Periplus

London

Illustration on previous page:
Terracotta head of the
Punic goddess Tanit.

© Roger Wood/CORBIS

Acknowledgements

We would like particularly to thank the following people and organisations for their help and contribution to this book:

Anastasia Anagnostopoulou Paloubis, president of the Hellenic Maritime Museum;
Laura Lionetti Barton of Odyssey Marine Exploration;
Maître Lucien Basch;
Prof. George F. Bass, Deborah N. Carlson and Ralph K. Pedersen, Institute of Nautical Archeology (INA);
Tom Boyd;
Prof. James A. Dengate, University of Illinois;
Aikaterini Dellaporta, Director of the Ephorate of Underwater Antiquities, Greece;
Honor Frost, Fellow of the Society of Antiquaries;
Itamar Grinberg, photographer;
Prof. Michael Jameson, director of the Halieis Project;
Dr Yaacov Kahanov, University of Haïfa;
Dr Karl Kilinski, Southern Methodist University;
Dr Elisha Linder, University of Haïfa;
Prof. Yannos Lolos, Dr Yannis Vichos, Dr Dimitris Kourkoumelis and Angeliki Simossi, Hellenic Institute of Marine Archaeology (HIMA);
Bjørn Lovén, director of the Zea Harbour Project;
National Archaeological Museum, Greece;
Dr Iván Negueruela, director of the Museo Nacional de Arqueología Marítima y Centro Nacional de Investigaciones Arqueológicas Submarinas, Cartagena;
Catherine A. Offinger, Institute for Exploration;
Prof. Karl M. Petruso, University of Texas at Arlington;
Prof. Lawrence E. Stager, Harvard University, Dorot Professor of the Archaeology of Israel, Director of the Semitic Museum;
Saint-Joseph University, Beirut;
Dr Michael Wedde;
and Michael Wright, The Science Museum, London.

Master seafarers
the Phoenicians and the Greeks

	Introduction	ix
I.	**The Phoenicians**	1
	A mysterious people	1
	Harbour sites	10
	Motya	11
	Tyre and Sidon	13
	Shipwrecks	21
	Cape Gelidonya	26
	Tanit and Elissa	34
	Mazarron 1 and 2	41
	Ma'agan Mikhael	50
	Melkarth	56
	Isola Lunga	58
II.	*Thalassa*, **the Greek sea**	63
	The odyssey of a people	65
	Harbour sites	76
	Halieis	76
	Samos	82
	Thassos	84
	Piraeus	89
	Shipwrecks	98
	Dokos	98
	Point Iria	105
	Alonnisos	112
	Tektas Burnu	118
	Kyrenia	122
	Antikythera	127
	Conclusion	133
	Glossary	135
	Bibliography	145

Introduction

Phoenician civilisation is shrouded in mystery, while the Greek legacy of literature, philosophy and art is fundamental to western culture. The works of Homer and Sophocles belong to the international literary canon, while not a single Phoenician papyrus, even a copy or a translation, has survived. Paradoxically, the Phoenicians gave us the rudiments of our alphabet. While Greek is an Indo-European language, Phoenician belonged to the Semitic languages, a group that includes Aramaic, Hebrew, Arabic and Punic, the dialect spoken in Carthage.

The Phoenicians and the Greeks appear at first glance to have had very little in common. But the influence these two cultures had on each other embraced the artistic, religious and economic domains.

Looking at the coastline of Phoenicia (modern-day Lebanon), it is easy to see why its inhabitants took to the sea. Hemmed in by hostile neighbours, their greatest geographical asset was access to the Mediterranean.

Geography alone does not, however, explain how the Phoenicians came to occupy the lands surrounding the Mediterranean, from its easternmost tip to the far west. They travelled to Spain and beyond, as far afield as the Gulf of Guinea, West Africa, and the British Isles. It is too often forgotten that the phenomenon of maritime colonisation predates the Hellenistic and Roman eras.

The Phoenicians' interest in trade, which began as far back as 1200 BC, was undoubtedly their motivation for venturing across the Mediterranean. The decline of Mycenaean commerce made possible the development of a regional Phoenician economy. Greek authors disparaged the Phoenicians as a merchant people, who preferred the exchange of goods to war. In ancient literature and even today, they are depicted unflatteringly as greedy, willing to do anything for a sale.

Phoenician merchantmen hugged the coasts by day, pulling into harbours for the night. Although Phoenician sailors also ventured on the open seas, it was this type of coastal navigation that led to the establishment of small trading posts which would eventually develop into fully-fledged cities.

Phoenician harbours around the Mediterranean reveal a distinctive design, apparently modelled on their builders' hometowns. André Parrot observes that, "The Phoenicians settled mainly on small coastal islands or promontories; in general, places with a gently shelving shore or in lagoons. These conditions provided shelter from the wind and the ability to safely accommodate shallow draught vessels. A Phoenician site is recognisable by its structure: small islands, such as Arados, Tyre (before being joined to the continent), Motya, Sulcis, Cadiz and others; and promontories, such as Sidon, Acra, Carthage, and Tharros."

Just as the Greeks colonised Italy in their search for Etruscan iron, the Phoenicians headed west in search of scarce metals. Evidence of Phoenician settlements has been found in Algeria at Hippo Regius (present day Annaba), Cirta (Constantine), Icosium (Algiers) and on Rachgoun island, most of which date from the 4th and 3rd centuries BC, long after the founding of Carthage, and in Morocco at Tamuda, Tangier and Lixus, dating from the 8th and 7th centuries BC.

These towns represented strategic points on the metal trade routes. This trade also led the Phoenicians to Spain, where it is generally agreed they founded Cadiz (Gadir in ancient times). Gold, silver, iron, tin and lead could be bought at low prices from Iberian mines and resold at great profit in the east, but not without risks. The Mazarron 2 wreck, found in southern Spain, was filled to the gunwales with lead ingots – a witness to the inherent dangers of carrying such a heavy cargo. But the Phoenicians were not intimidated by the sea, and came to dominate Sardinia, Malta, Ibiza and Sicily.

Western Phoenicia emerged as a discrete entity in 814 BC with the founding of Carthage, whose citizens continued the Phoenician traditions of trade and exploration. An account of the Carthaginian Hanno's periplus to West Africa survives in a Greek translation of a Punic inscription. This remarkable text begins, "A record of the voyage of King Hanno of Carthage, round the lands of Libya which lie beyond the Pillars of Hercules, is engraved on tablets hung in the Temple of Baal, as follows..."

A century later came another great wave of colonisation. Hellenic people settled in Asia Minor, on the fringes of the Black Sea and around the Mediterranean. These Greek settlements differed in nature to the Phoenician colonies, but exchanges were intense between the communities and the two cultures exerted a strong influence on one another.

Art, in all its forms, is the clearest illustration of this reciprocal influence. The Greek Orientalising period owes much to Phoenician production processes, since Greek artists often worked for Phoenician clients, especially from the 4th century BC. Greek marbles became popular along the coast of Phoenicia. These were used as sarcophagi for Phoenician aristocrats in imitation of their kings, who were in turn inspired by the Egyptians. This burial fashion would also later be adopted by the Romans.

During the Geometric period (9th century BC), the Greek language spread to all sections of Phoenician society, and many Phoenicians adopted a Greek name. Even the most famous of Phoenician industries, glass-making, felt the effects of Greek influence.

The first contact between the Greeks and the Phoenicians unfolded in a climate of mutual co-operation and cultural exchange. But when the people of the Aegean spread across southern Italy and Sicily in proximity to Phoenician trading posts, rivalries emerged which had developed into open conflict by the 6th century BC. Unlike the mother city of Tyre, Carthage possessed a powerful army. At Alalia (modern-day Aleria), in around 535 BC, the Carthaginians and their Etruscan allies drove the Greeks from Corsica and ensured their domination of the western Mediterranean. Four troubled centuries ensued, with battles fought in the Aegean and the Mediterranean between the Greeks and Phoenicians, Greeks and Persians, and the Carthaginians and Romans.

The sea has left little trace of these naval battles, whereas numerous merchant shipwrecks have been discovered, providing archaeologists with invaluable information on the maritime history of these master seafarers.

I. The Phoenicians

The name 'Phoenician' comes from the Greek word *phoenikes*, meaning 'purple', and was given to these traders because of their expertise in producing dye of this colour from murex shells.

The Phoenicians inhabited the Syro-Palestinian coast from the Gulf of Issus in the north to Mount Carmel in the south. Although closely related to the Canaanites and Aramaeans, their exact origin continues to be debated. They referred to themselves as Canaanites because their Semitic ancestors had settled in the land of Canaan (modern day Palestine). The Greeks called them Sidonians in reference to Sidon, one of Phoenicia's main cities, as well as Carthaginians.

These designations reflect a sense of belonging to a particular city rather than to a state. This is because Phoenicia never evolved either into a nation or an empire. Instead, it remained a collection of politically autonomous city-states, each governed by its own king, which were in continual competition with one another and only formed occasional alliances in order to resist invaders.

1. A mysterious people

In the 3rd millennium BC, Semitic peoples appeared all along the coast of present-day Lebanon. They were influenced by a number of civilisations such

Terracotta model of an ancient Phoenician ship.

© photo RMN: Franck Raux

Master seafarers

Bas-relief of a Phoenician merchant ship known as the Boat of Tarsus, from the 1st century BC.

© Gianni Dagli Orti/CORBIS

as the Hittites, Hourrites and Egyptians, as well as the Cretans and Mycenaeans, the two seafaring peoples that dominated the Aegean area during the 2nd millennium BC. Phoenicia reached its zenith between the 13th and 8th centuries BC, during which period three areas rose to prominence: Tyre in the south, Arvad-Simyra in the north and in the middle, Sidon, Berytus and Byblos.

Egypt showed an early interest in Byblos, which was the trading and religious capital of the Phoenician coastal area between 2000 and 1500 BC. Sidon, a small fishing town during the 3rd millennium BC, grew powerful, vying with the other two main cities for naval superiority throughout the 2nd millennium BC. It then became a protectorate of Tyre, the main Phoenician city from 1200 BC, when the Canaanite cities broke free from Egyptian rule and enjoyed a period of independence.

Tyre developed maritime and trade relations throughout the Mediterranean world, its prestige enhanced by the alliances which its king, Hiram I (early 10th century BC), forged with King Solomon of Israel, and by its numerous colonies, including the city of Carthage in North Africa.

Unlike the Greeks, the Phoenicians left behind few traces of their presence, apart from a few inscriptions, and therefore we know virtually nothing about their daily life.

Two factors account for this lack of evidence. The first is related to the weather. Like the Egyptians, the Phoenicians wrote on papyrus scrolls, which deteriorated over time due to the region's moist climate. In addition, bad weather gradually wore away stone inscriptions until they became unreadable. The second factor stems from the political reality of the age. Phoenician cities possessed an opening on to the sea, the envy of their landlocked rivals. Without a merchant fleet of their own, the Assyrians and Babylonians were quick to invade, pillage, sack and then rebuild Phoenician cities.

A few items made in Phoenicia, as well as frescoes with invaluable images of their cities and ships, have been uncovered during archaeological excavations in Mesopotamia, Egypt, Cyprus and elsewhere, as well as a few wall fragments, some tombs and temple foundations. Archaeologists working on land, however, were forced to admit that Phoenician ruins were few and far between, and that it was difficult to distinguish them from the remains left by invaders.

To better understand Phoenician life and history, they were forced to rely on accounts from neighbouring peoples, and in particular on Greek writings and the Bible, which depict Phoenicians as matchless navigators, bold adventurers and shrewd traders. Homer saw them as "mariners renowned, greedy merchantmen, with countless gauds in a black ship".

More recently, the discovery and study of Phoenician and Carthaginian wrecks has made it possible to increase our knowledge of this people – and give credence to the concept of Phoenicians as the greatest navigators of their time.

Phoenician figurine.

© David Lees/CORBIS

Phoenician gold pendant.

© David Lees/CORBIS

Cornwall
Atlantic Ocean
Gaul
Iberia
Massilia
Balearic Islands
Huelva
Gadir
Toscanos
Carthage
Phoenician maritime routes
Legend
important towns
Phoenician ports
Phoenician settlements
trading routes

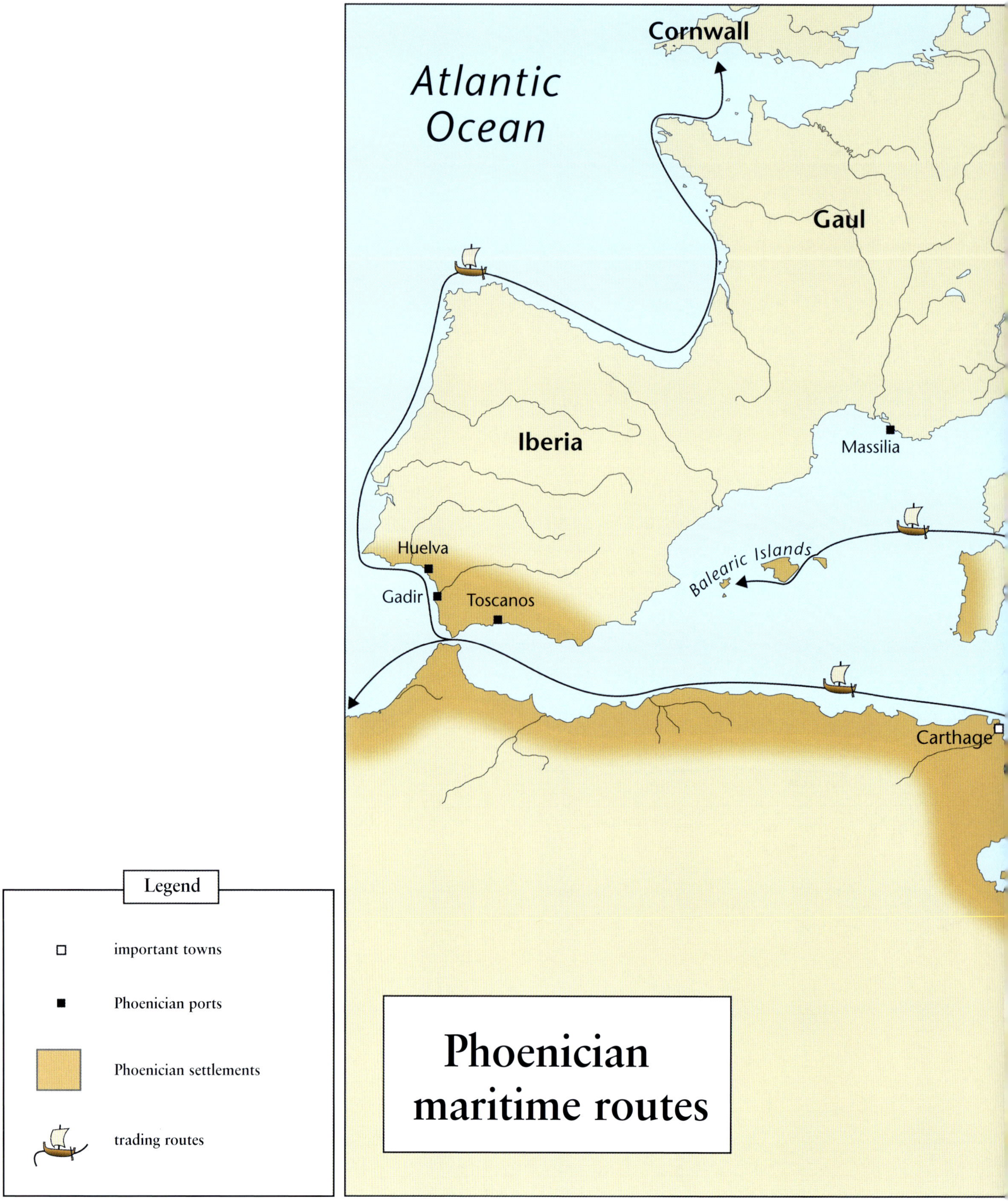

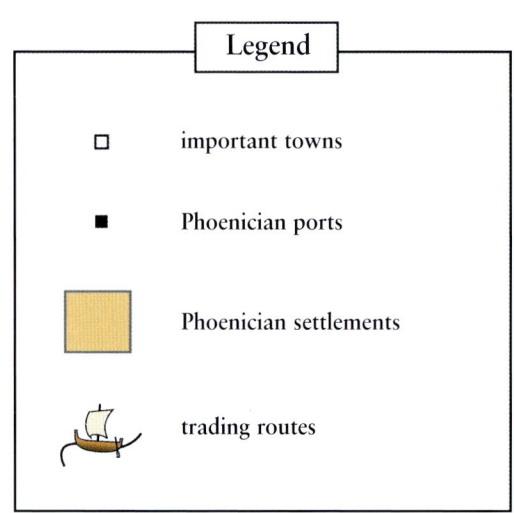

I. The Phoenicians

Chronology of the Phoenicians

The oldest dates are approximate – new archaeological discoveries are constantly revising our knowledge of the ancient world.

circa 7000 BC: first traces of settlers at Byblos.

3000-2900 BC: first dwellings at Byblos.

2900 BC: the Egyptian king Snefrou (last of the 3rd Dynasty) dispatches a naval expedition in search of cedar wood from Phoenicia.

2750 BC: foundation of Tyre.

2100 BC: conquest of Byblos by the Amorrites.

2000-1500 BC: Byblos becomes the religious and commercial capital of the Phoenician coast.

1200 BC: Phoenician coast is invaded from the sea as Tyrian navigators explore the Mediterranean. Canaanite settlers on the Syro-Palestinian coast become known as Phoenicians.

1110 BC: beginning of the Phoenician golden age and ocean voyages. Tyrians found Gadir (Cadiz).

1100-700 BC: Phoenician sailors explore the furthest outposts of the Mediterranean.

1020 BC: beginning of the reign of Abibal, the earliest known king of Tyre.

1000 BC: the invention of the 22-letter alphabet. Tyrians set up towns at Cition, on the island of Cyprus, at Rhodes and in Crete.

1000-750 BC: period of wealth and naval expansion.

980 BC: Hiram I succeeds Abibal as king of Tyre.

circa 970 BC: according to the Bible, Tyre trades with 'Tarshish' in the far western Mediterranean and their ships carry gold to King Solomon of Tyre.

880-630 BC: Phoenicia gradually becomes an Assyrian protectorate.

821 BC: foundation of Kambia by the Sidonians in the Gulf of Tunis.

814 BC: foundation of Carthage by the fugitive Tyrians.

734 BC: the Greeks begin to establish colonies in Sicily.

circa 720 BC: the Carthaginians establish Motya, in western Sicily.

681 BC: Sidon and Tyre come under Assyrian rule.

654 BC: the Carthaginians establish Ebussus (Ibiza).

circa 600 BC: the Carthaginians and the Etruscans unite against Greece.

586-573 BC: siege and destruction of Tyre by Nebuchadnezzar II, king of Babylon. Tyre remains under Babylonian control until 572 BC.

circa 550 BC: the Carthaginian general Magon defeats the Greeks in Sicily.

539 BC: taking of Babylon by Cyrus the Persian. Return of prosperity to Phoenician ports.

535 BC: naval victory of Phoenicia over the Phocaeans at Alalia, off Corsica.

494 BC: first Median war between Persia and Greece. The Phoenicians lend naval assistance to Persia.

480 BC: battle of Salamine. The Persians, fighting with help from Phoenician ships, are defeated by the Greeks. Greeks also defeat the Carthaginians at Himera, in Sicily.

430 BC: Hanno, the famous Carthaginian navigator, makes his great voyage.

397 BC: the Greeks lay siege to Motya, destroying the town.

350 BC: Artaxerxes III, king of Persia, attacks Sidon.

336 BC: Alexander the Great begins his conquest of the Near East.

333 BC: Alexander takes Byblos and Sidon and lays siege to Tyre in the following year. Decline of eastern Phoenicia.

264-241 BC: first Punic war between Rome and Carthage.

228-229 BC: the Carthaginian Hasdrubal founds Carthago Nova (Cartagena) in Spain.

221 BC: Hasdrubal is assassinated. Hannibal the Great succeeds him.

218-202 BC: second Punic war, ending in the defeat of Carthage.

146 BC: third Punic war ends with Carthage defeated again. Decline of western Phoenicia.

The call of the sea

The Phoenicians were recognised as great pioneers of civilisation. Intrepid, ingenious and enterprising, they spread their vast knowledge of art, literature and shipbuilding throughout the Mediterranean region, avoiding the use of force where possible in favour of peaceful trading. They excelled in textile production and commerce, and in working with metal, wood, stone and glass.

The Phoenicians had no real option but to turn to the sea. Phoenicia only occupied a small coastal strip between 12km and 50km wide. The Hittites had wrested control of the northern Syrian coast from them. The Philistines had taken possession of the coast to the south. And to the east, Phoenicia was cut off by a mountain range. What remained was a tiny area composed of heavily populated cities and deprived of arable land and raw materials, except for the much-prized cedar wood from their hinterland.

To survive, the Phoenicians were forced to import provisions in exchange for a few luxury commodities. The type of trade practised by the Phoenicians is explained in two biblical passages. In 1 Kings, Solomon asks Hiram, king of Tyre, to provide him with cedar in exchange for which he promises to send foodstuffs.

Hiram sends this reply to Solomon: "I have received your message. In this matter of timber, both cedar and pine, I will do all you wish.

"My men shall bring down the logs from Lebanon to the sea and I will make them up into rafts to be floated to the place you appoint; I will have them broken up and you can remove them. You, on your part, will meet my wishes if you provide the food for my household."

So Hiram kept Solomon supplied with all the cedar and pine that he wanted, and Solomon supplied Hiram annually with 6,000 tonnes of wheat as food for his household and 8,000 litres of finest olive oil.

In 2 Chronicles, Solomon, who is eager to build a magnificent temple adorned with gold, silver and rich fabrics, once again appeals to Hiram and repeats his promise to furnish provisions:

"Send me then a skilled craftsman, a man able to work in gold and silver, copper and iron, and in purple, crimson and violet yarn, who is also an expert engraver [...] Send me also cedar, pine, and algum timber from Lebanon [...]

"I will supply provisions for your servants, the woodmen who fell the trees: 6,000 tonnes of wheat and 6,000 of barley, with 20,000 bath of wine and 800,000 litres of oil."

The Phoenicians responded to demand by working with metals, producing shimmering, brightly coloured fabrics and supplying the cedar that was much sought-after elsewhere. They first expanded their commerce via overland trade routes, such as the caravan route from Tyre to Egypt. These merchants succeeded in exploiting their key position at the crossroads between east and west in order to obtain a large number of tradable commodities, cultivating, for example, good relations with the east because of its spices and precious gems.

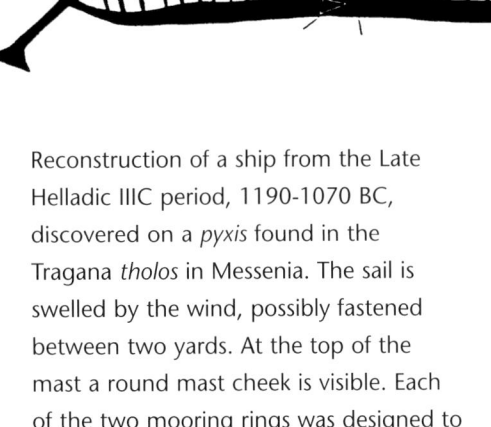

Reconstruction of a ship from the Late Helladic IIIC period, 1190-1070 BC, discovered on a *pyxis* found in the Tragana *tholos* in Messenia. The sail is swelled by the wind, possibly fastened between two yards. At the top of the mast a round mast cheek is visible. Each of the two mooring rings was designed to secure a halyard. Of the four lines running from the mast cheek to the prow, two are guy ropes and the other two are halyards. One is attached half-way between the poop and the mast, while the other is secured near the helmsman. A large forecastle is formed by horizontal and vertical beams and crossbeams. Homer refers to this construction as an *ikria* in *The Iliad* and *The Odyssey*.

© Georges S. Korres, 'New observations on the ship representation of the LH IIIC', Tropis I. Redrawn in ink by Michael Wedde

I. The Phoenicians

At the end of the 2nd millennium BC, the Phoenicians turned to the sea and built harbours. In search of new markets, they gradually established footholds throughout the Mediterranean region.

Trading with the Greeks, the Phoenicians established colonies and trading centres in the eastern and western Mediterranean; in Cyprus (where Phoenician inscriptions have been found), Malta, Sicily, Sardinia, the Balearic islands and southern Spain. They brought to these fertile regions, rich in minerals and precious metals, their famous cedar, spices, purple dye, and exquisite, costly *objets d'art* – ivory carvings and glassware – made from raw materials and precious metals they had imported.

As masters of the art of navigation, they were the first to venture into the Atlantic ocean and to find their bearings using the North Star, which the Greeks called the Phoenician Star. The oldest Phoenician trading centre was established at Gadir in 1110 BC, followed by Utica, a North African city north-west of Carthage, in 1101 BC. However, the lack of irrefutable proof means that archaeologists can only put forward hypotheses about these colonies. The first tangible evidence of Phoenician occupation dates from the 8th century BC.

The Phoenicians also traded with Egypt and established themselves along the North African coastline. In order to escape their Assyrian conquerors, the inhabitants of Tyre fled to a more hospitable region and founded Carthage (which means 'new city') in 814 BC. Their search for metal and mineral ores even led them into the Atlantic ocean, along the coastline of Gaul and as far as Cornwall.

They were able to reach the western Mediterranean via three routes. By the first, they sailed along the northern coastline and then that of Greece to get to Corfu. From there, they headed on to Sicily. By the second, they followed the African coast from Egypt as far as Morocco. Phoenician mariners also braved the open sea, calling at Cyprus, Crete, Malta, Sicily, Sardinia and the Balearic islands.

Pendant in the form of a Phoenician boat, dating from 404-399 BC.

© Gianni Dagli Orti/CORBIS

2. Harbour sites

There were two types of harbours in Phoenicia – those built on estuaries, such as Byblos and Al Mina, and those formed by small islands opposite the coastline, such as Tyre and Sidon. On the routes leading to the West, the Phoenicians chose to berth their ships in similar sites – inland ports or offshore islands.

Numerous traces of Phoenician harbour installations have been discovered in estuaries along the Mediterranean, for example at Huelva and Toscanos on the Iberian Peninsula, at Bitai and Tosa in Sardinia, and along the North African coast at Utica and Rachgoun. Replicas of the harbours at Tyre and Sidon can be found in Algiers, Mogador and Cadiz.

The Phoenicians constructed artificial harbours by transforming these natural refuges into elaborate structures composed of jetties, quays and dock areas. There are few traces left to testify to their ingenuity, but what remains shows the Phoenicians were the first great harbour builders.

The remains of the northern port on the island of Motya off the east coast of Sicily.
© Giuseppe Leone

Sacrifice area on the island of Motya.
© David Lees/CORBIS

The first artificial harbours in the Mediterranean – Motya

At the end of the 8th century BC, the Carthaginians settled in Motya, a tiny island east of Sicily, in order to oppose the expansion of Greek colonisation into this part of the Mediterranean. They fortified Motya and built a great wall, 9m high, flanked by towers which totally surrounded the island.

The Greeks destroyed the town in 397 BC and the site was never reconstructed. This was a stroke of luck for the archaeologists, who found themselves with a purely Phoenician site which, unlike Carthage, had not been built over by the Greeks or Romans. Discovered in 1619, Motya was the subject of trial excavations at the end of the 19th century. It was excavated between 1907 and 1926 by the Whitaker team, who unearthed the wall and other structures, and later by Italian and British archaeologists.

The Phoenicians reached the island via the north gate, which was protected by two huge square bastions and had three entrances opening onto a jetty leading to the Sicilian mainland. A necropolis was discovered in the north of the island. Several hundred cremation burial sites were excavated and iron weapons, jewellery, Carthaginian vases and Greek pottery were unearthed. The *temenos* (sacred enclosure adjacent to a temple) of Cappiddazzu, located near the gate, contained a three-aisled edifice adorned by a cornice with Egyptian moulding. A small temple with a square altar had been erected nearby, as well as a *tophet* (a place for idolatrous worship and sacrifice) containing thousands of urns. More

The basin of the *cothon* in the town's southern port. The quays and numerous blocks of stone are visible, designed to harbour Phoenician ships.

© Giuseppe Leone

than a thousand steles bearing the effigy of idols were identified. Roughly 40 of these had inscriptions and were dedicated to the god Baal Hammon. The *tophet* also produced a grimacing mask, some imported Punic statuettes and a terracotta female protome. Two pottery workshops complete with kilns were also found in the north of Motya. In one of them, murex shell fragments were discovered, indicating that the Phoenicians manufactured purple dye on the island.

Ships entered via the south gate, into the *cothon*, a huge enclosed dock area dug out of the coastline and connected to the sea by a channel. Examples of this type of *cothon* have been identified in Carthage and Utica.

The channel itself was located inside the town's fortifications, thereby affording ships a greater degree of protection. It was 5m wide and bordered by stone blocks. Some of these had holes, where beams once fitted to hold ships while they were being repaired. In addition, the floor of the channel was paved and had a groove down the centre, possibly to allow keels to pass through. The *cothon* itself was 50m long and 35m wide, with a maximum depth of 9m, and surrounded by gravel quays used for unloading goods.

The harbour at Motya is one of only a few examples of Phoenician *cothons* and by far the best preserved. This type of construction was not found on the Syro-Palestinian coast, which suggests that it was used exclusively by the western Phoenicians.

Two harbour cities: Tyre and Sidon

Throughout this period, Tyre and Sidon vied alternately for glory. When Sidon was in the spotlight, Tyre was relegated to obscurity. When Tyre was making its influence felt, Sidon was overshadowed. Sidon, which the Bible calls the 'mother of Phoenician cities', was the first to achieve wealth and become a famous Phoenician port. So great was Sidon's renown that Homer and Virgil made it synonymous with Phoenicia as a whole. Although Homer was certainly familiar with Byblos and Tyre, which overshadowed Sidon from the 10th century BC onwards, his verses recall the time when Sidon was at the pinnacle of its fame and influence. He evokes a thriving city with a flourishing craft industry, commerce and fleet which dominated sea traffic on the Mediterranean. Following a period of decline, Sidon's influence was rekindled during the Persian era after Tyre had been besieged by the Babylonians in the 6th century BC.

Meanwhile, leadership gradually passed to Tyre, which emerged as the most powerful city in Phoenicia. The Tyrians acquired a large fleet and ventured even further afield than their Sidonian predecessors, reaching Cadiz, Cornwall and Carthage. Trade with their colonies flourished. The city itself bustled with activity and was packed with artisans and merchants. Nowadays, the ancient harbour lies completely submerged.

Excavations at Tyre

The city of Tyre was situated on a rocky islet 600m from the shore. In the Phoenicians' time, the island was joined to the mainland by a ford which Alexander the Great transformed into a sea wall in 332 BC.

Archaeologists began to excavate Tyre as early as the 19th century, eager to unearth this wealthy city so highly praised by Ezekiel, though detailed underwater exploration did not exist at the time. It was the archaeologist Antoine Poidebard who would later discover the submerged remains of Tyre's two ancient harbours using aerial photography, a method first employed by Paul Vega in 1927.

Detail from one of the bronze bands from the gates at Balawat in northern Iraq depicting ships off the island of Tyre, carrying gifts to Shalmaneser III (the island is to the left).

© The British Museum

Ezekiel (ch. 27: 3-11): Lament for Tyre

In his famous lament, Ezekiel evokes the legendary wealth of Tyre before it was besieged for 13 years by Nebuchadnezzar's troops between 586 and 573 BC. He describes Tyre using the allegory of a magnificent ship made from priceless materials imported from far and wide. His words emphasise the sheer scale of Tyrian commercial ventures and the wealth and opulence of a city so rich in widely tradable commodities.

O Tyre, you said, 'I am perfect in beauty'.
Your frontiers are on the high seas,
your builders made your beauty perfect;
they fashioned all your timbers of pine from Senir;
they took a cedar from Lebanon
to raise up a mast over you.
They made your oars
of oaks from Bashan;
they made your decks strong
with boxwood from the coasts of Kittim.
Your canvas was linen,
patterned linen from Egypt
to make your sails visible from afar;
your awnings were violet and purple
from the coasts of Elishah,
to keep your wares safe;
men of Sidon and Arvad
became your oarsmen;
you had skilled men within you, O Tyre,
who served as your helmsmen.
You had men from Gebal
with skill and experience
caulking your seams.
You had all seagoing ships
to market your wares,
and their sailors to buy your goods;
men of Pharas, Lud and Put,
served as warriors in your army;
they hung shield and helmet
from your rigging,
and it was they who gave you your glory.
Men of Arvad and Cilicia manned all your walls,
men of Gammad were posted on your towers;
they hung their shields from your walls.
It was they who made your beauty perfect.

I. The Phoenicians

The birth of a method

Exploration of the harbour at Tyre only began after a lengthy period of archival research. Poidebard relied particularly on biblical descriptions of the city and the travelogue in Strabo's *Geography*. Strabo indicates that the city had two harbours: a northern one within the city walls and a southern one, known as the 'Egyptian' port, outside the city walls. In addition, the works of Flavius Arrianus, written in the 2nd century AD and themselves based on historical texts, provided Poidebard and his team with an invaluable summary of the history of Tyre.

Could it be that remnants of these harbours, of which the ancients spoke so highly, still existed? Poidebard knew that this question could only be answered by an underwater investigation.

Unlike his predecessors, who had based their work solely on a study of ancient texts and had therefore been unable to map out the two harbours, Poidebard decided to carry out an aerial survey of the submerged site and conduct an underwater expedition led by a deep-sea diver.

Three series of excavations were organised between 1934 and 1936. Antoine Poidebard's observations are chronicled in his book *Tyr, un port phénicien disparu* (Tyre: a vanished Phoenician harbour). Although these findings have occasionally been challenged, his role as the pioneer of modern underwater harbour archaeology is undisputed.

Tyre, aerial view of the peninsula. In this photograph, the archaeological sites around the isthmus to the south of the town have not yet been excavated. The main tree-lined road of the isthmus is visible, as well as the sunken remains of the northern and southern ports.

© Saint-Joseph University, Oriental Library, Beirut
Photo: Antoine Poidebard

Master seafarers

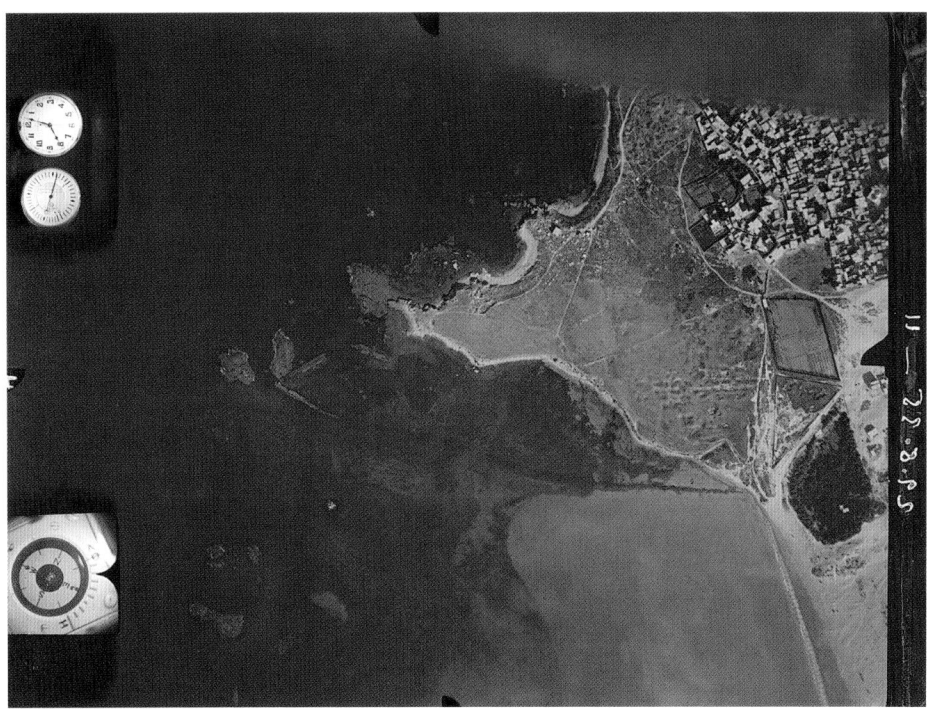

Aerial view of Tyre, showing the probable site of the 'Egyptian' port to the south.

© Saint-Joseph University, Oriental Library, Beirut
Photo: Antoine Poidebard

Aerial reconnaissance

In order to locate traces of the ancient ruins, Poidebard first carried out aerial reconnaissance, taking a series of photographs of the seabed. In spite of poor visibility due to murky water and sunlight reflecting on the surface, he was able to pinpoint the ruins and tell the diver which areas to explore.

These photographs, together with soundings and underwater observations, made it possible to draw up a preliminary map of the ancient site.

The role of the deep-sea diver

Once the ruins had been located, it was the turn of the deep-sea diver to explore the underwater archaeological site. There were numerous obstacles to overcome – the ruins were buried beneath blankets of seaweed and thick layers of sediment that had to be stripped away using a pick. His task was all the more difficult because the aqualung had not yet been invented. Poidebard's diver was equipped with a heavy helmet supplied with air from the surface via two feeder tubes. All this paraphernalia hampered his movement considerably, a problem compounded by the heavy swell which was ever-present during the excavation.

After the diver uncovered the objects, he had to take samples of certain material. The location of any artefact removed was carefully noted on the map and the samples were sent to a Paris laboratory for analysis. Back on the surface, the diver reported his observations and made rough sketches of the objects examined.

As it was difficult for him to judge distances under water, he had to carry out several dives at the same spot to verify his measurements. The diver wore goggles fitted with a lens designed to improve visibility at depths of up to 12m.

Underwater photography

Underwater photography was another method of checking and complementing the diver's observations. It was carried out from the surface by suspending a camera, which had to be fixed at 90° to prevent objects from appearing distorted. Complementing these surface pictures, were others taken underwater, using a small 9.5mm camera housed in a watertight body and later, in 1936, a more sophisticated, Leica camera. This 'double perspective' gave a clearer idea of the shape and dimensions of the ruins.

Outcome of the excavation: reconstruction of the two ports

The two harbours were a testament to the engineering genius of the Phoenicians. They formed a huge, carefully laid-out complex skilfully planned to provide shelter from the prevailing winds.

The northern harbour was composed of an 8m-thick mole which started from the wall tower located to the east of the modern day lighthouse. It was also protected by a natural barrier of partially exposed reefs stretching for 1600m and facing the northerly and westerly winds. It was impossible to tell from the diver's observations if the reefs had been converted into a breakwater.

The investigation in the southern harbour was more fruitful and revealed the overall architecture of the Egyptian harbour, whose southern and western limits were defined by two moles. The Phoenicians had built the main entrance to the harbour in the middle of the southern mole, which was 750m long and 8m thick.

Tyre, underwater view of divers at work.

© Saint-Joseph University, Oriental Library, Beirut
Photo: Antoine Poidebard

Diver taking a photograph using an early underwater camera in the southern port of Tyre.

© Saint-Joseph University, Oriental Library, Beirut
Photo: Antoine Poidebard

The angle made by the junction of the two moles formed a spur which provided effective protection from the westerly and south-westerly winds. They were constructed from rectangular stone blocks laid with the short end facing outwards. An impressive tower had been built between the western mole and the ancient city wall.

The Egyptian harbour was made up of several docking areas. The western section had two, one polygonal and the other rectangular. Searches in this area revealed the remains of a quay surrounded by stone walls. Although the upper part dates from the Roman period, the foundations are older and almost certainly Phoenician. The eastern section contained two docking areas, one polygonal and another square. Here again the ruins of a quay were discovered.

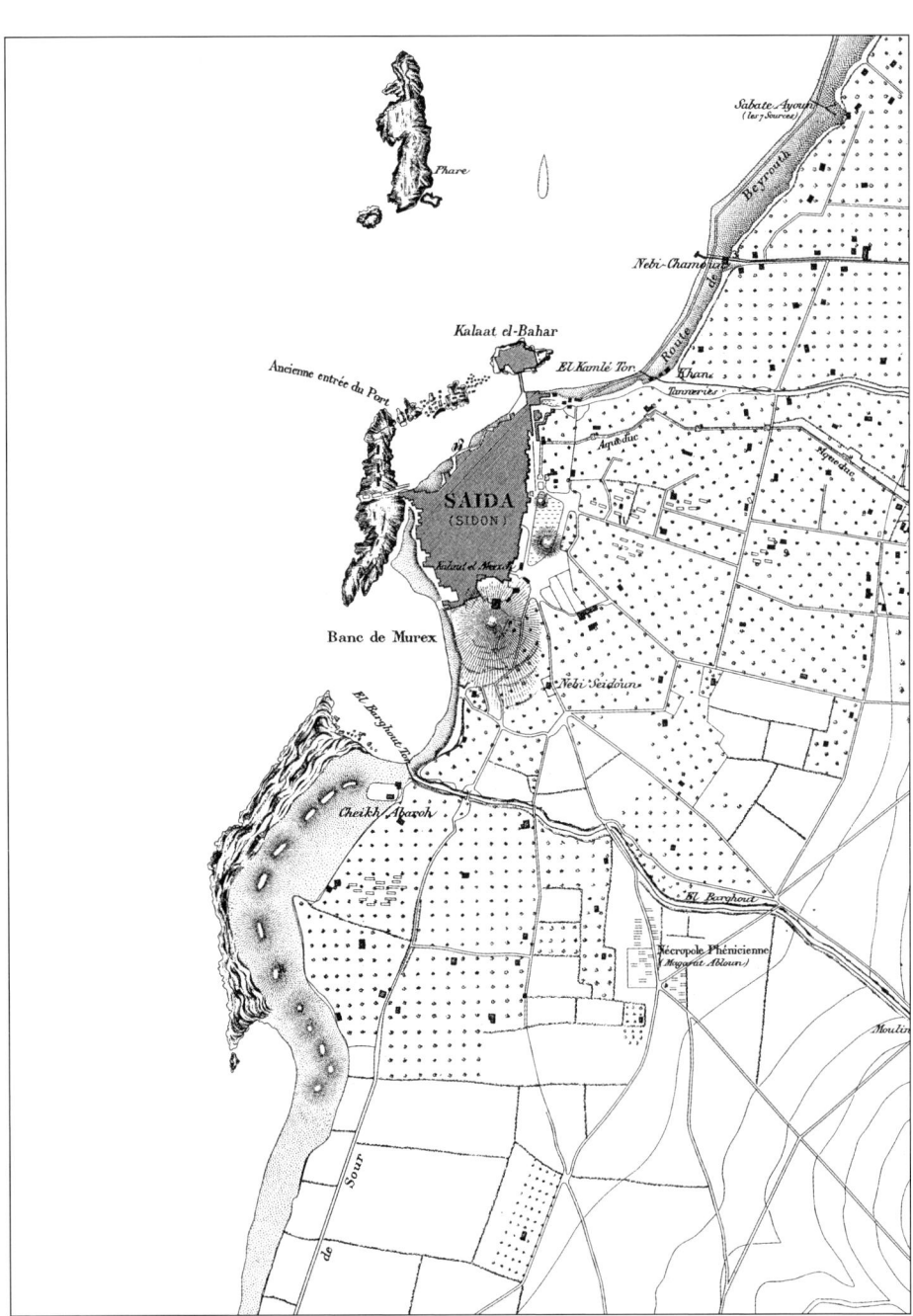

Map showing the coastline and the archaeological excavation at the ancient port of Sidon.

Map taken from *Une Nécropole royale à Sidon*, O. Hamdy Bey, T. Reinach, Paris, 1892

I. The Phoenicians

The moles were not the harbour's only protection against the winds and the waves: about 2km offshore, a natural harbour was created by three barrier reefs which were enlarged using stone blocks. This use of reefs is found in other Phoenician ports such as Rouad and Sidon.

The excavation of Sidon

During the Phoenician period, the city of Sidon was perched on a small promontory between two harbours: a natural basin to the south and an enclosed northern harbour. Antoine Poidebard excavated the site between 1946 and 1950, using the same methods of aerial and underwater exploration as at Tyre. He recorded his observations in a book entitled *Sidon, l'aménagement du Port antique* (Sidon: layout of the ancient harbour).

Distinguishing the Phoenician structures from earlier constructions proved more difficult here than at Tyre, as the city had undergone numerous phases of reconstruction, in particular during the Persian, Hellenistic and medieval periods. It is possible that those who came after the Phoenicians did not destroy their handiwork, but merely improved and enlarged upon it. What is clear, however, is that certain sections of the harbours date from before the Phoenician period.

The layout of the northern harbour, made up of two ports, was similar to that in Tyre, offering protection from the wind and waves, and preventing it from silting up. A natural barrier of reefs ensured protection to the west. Too low in parts to act as an effective windbreak, it had been raised by adding a wall and made into quays. To the north and east, the harbour was protected by two moles. The northern one, which began at the northernmost limit of the natural barrier,

Sidon: aerial view of the entrance to the northern port showing the mole built to protect the northern port and to reinforce the natural seawall.

© Saint-Joseph University, Oriental Library, Beirut
Photo: Antoine Poidebard 1936

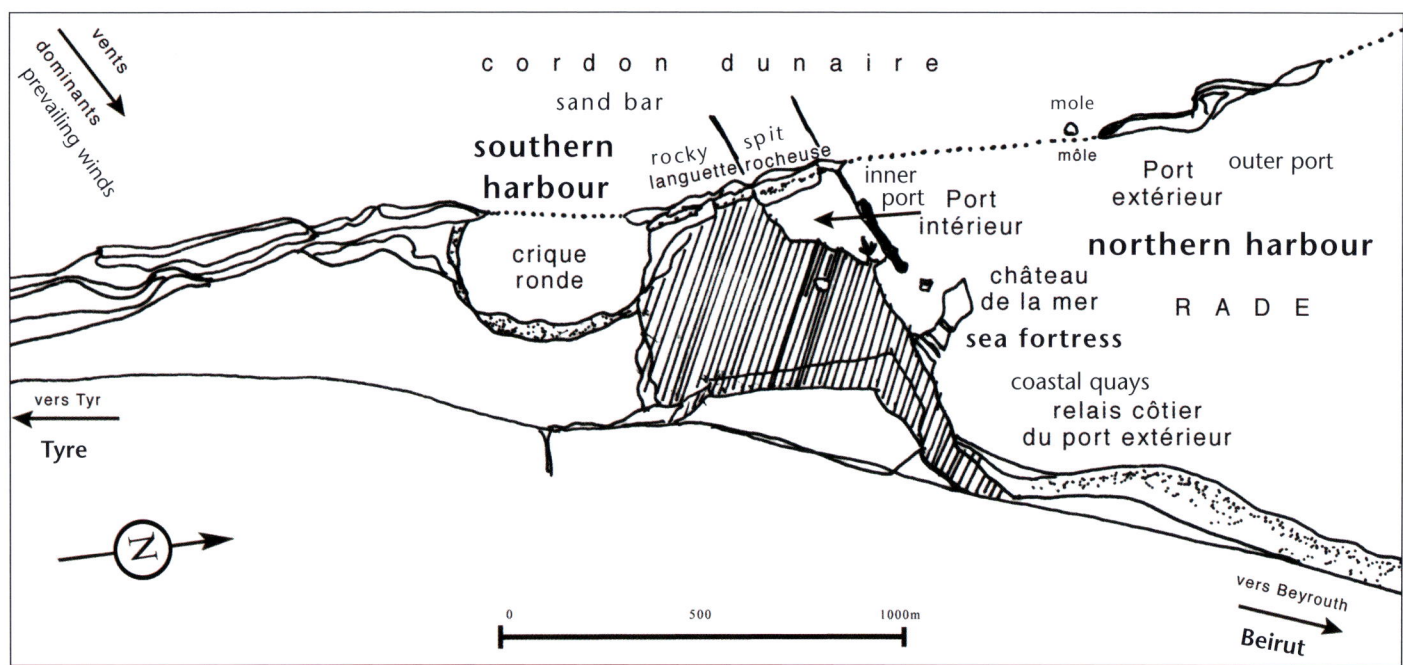

General map of Sidon from the 1940s excavation, showing the Phoenician engineers' skilful use of natural features.

© Poidebard and J. Lauffray

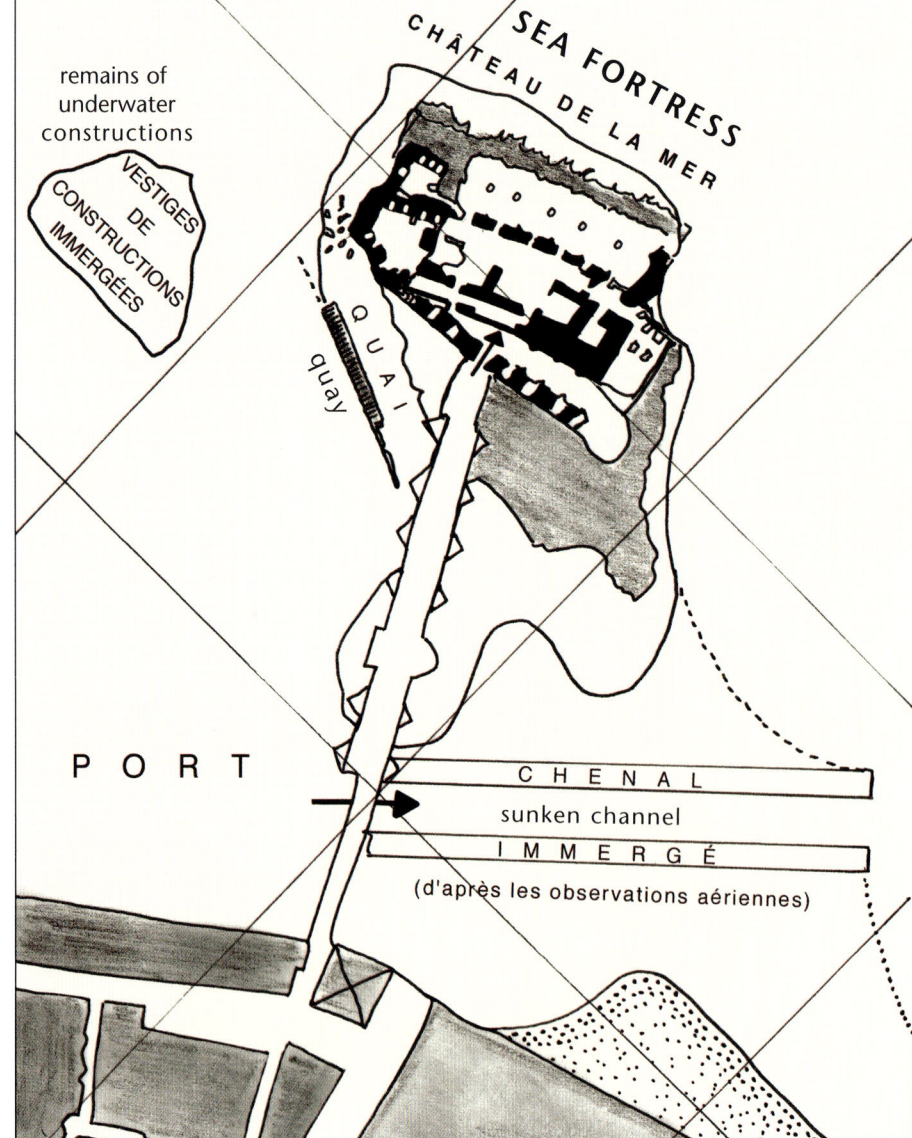

Map of the sea fortress at Sidon based on aerial reconnaissance.

© Poidebard and J. Lauffray

stretched for 230m and was extended by a jetty. Some remnants suggest that watchtowers had been built around the moles to protect the harbour from enemy attacks.

The southern harbour had been laid out in similar fashion to protect against the wind and rough seas. It had a mole running perpendicular to the shore. An 8m wide gap between the mole and the shore served as the harbour entrance. The mole itself was used as a quay. However, as its 50m length was insufficient to accommodate the sizeable Phoenician fleet, the shoreline was also laid out with quays. More than 30 mooring posts were identified, all predating the Roman period and again almost certainly Phoenician.

Whether at Motya, Tyre or Sidon, or even the few Phoenician ruins found in the ancient harbour at Carthage, these sites all indicate that the Phoenicians had mastered the technique of harbour construction at a much earlier date then was previously thought, and knew how to protect themselves from the prevailing winds, the power of the sea, silt and enemy attacks.

3. Shipwrecks

Until the middle of the 20th century, our knowledge of how naval architecture evolved in Antiquity was based on representations of ships on frescoes, vases, coins and other ancient artefacts. Since then, the discovery of wrecks dating from the Bronze and Iron Ages has helped to make this knowledge more accurate.

Underwater excavation has revealed more merchant ships than warships, since warships, being lighter, sank less frequently and when they were disabled in combat, the victors made every effort to salvage them; if this proved impossible, the vessels were left to run aground. Without heavy cargo and made of timber that was extremely quick to rot, they therefore disappeared without trace.

Illustrations of Canaanite and Minoan ships depict almost identical types of vessels. A Minoan seal from the 2nd millennium BC displaying a very wide ship with fixed rigging in the centre of the hull confirms the resemblance between Minoan and Phoenician craft.

The Canaanites acquired advanced boat-building techniques from the Cretans, with whom they traded frequently. These same techniques would later

This pottery fragment from the Late Geometric I, c. 760-735 BC, was removed clandestinely from the Kerameikos cemetery during the late 19th century and ended up in the Louvre.

© Lucien Basch, The Institute for the Preservation of Nautical Tradition

be used by the Phoenicians, Greeks and Romans, and the so-called 'shell-first' method is still in use today in the construction of traditional fishing boats. This involves carpenters assembling the keel and the hull first, followed by the ribs and the deck beams. Once the ship's framework was assembled, they added the outer planking used to support the upper deck, finally laying the planking on the inside and caulking the hull with oakum. The boards and planking were held together with mortise-and-tenon joints and metal nails.

Phoenician ships were built from the hard, resistant wood mentioned in Ezekiel's lament: cedar, cypress and oak. Pine and fir were reserved for non-structural sections, such as the cabin and the large apotropaic eyes carved or drawn on either side of the prow, intended to help ships 'see' their route more clearly and avert potential danger.

Ships were regarded as living beings and as such received great care and attention. The launch of a warship, for example, involved a rather gruesome ceremony: classical authors tell of prisoners being crushed beneath the hull so that the ship would be spared further bloodletting.

Warships and trading vessels

In time of war, speed and manoeuvrability were of paramount importance for any vessel. Consequently, carpenters built ships that were light and long enough to accommodate a large number of soldiers and sailors. They preferred to use oars for increased speed and only employed sails to steer the vessel. The stern was similar to that of merchant ships although the prow differed markedly. It

Wooden model of a penteconter.

© Hellenic Maritime Museum

I. The Phoenicians

Reconstruction of a Punic ship
in plan, elevation and cross-section.

© Punic Ship Mission; drawing by Michael Leek

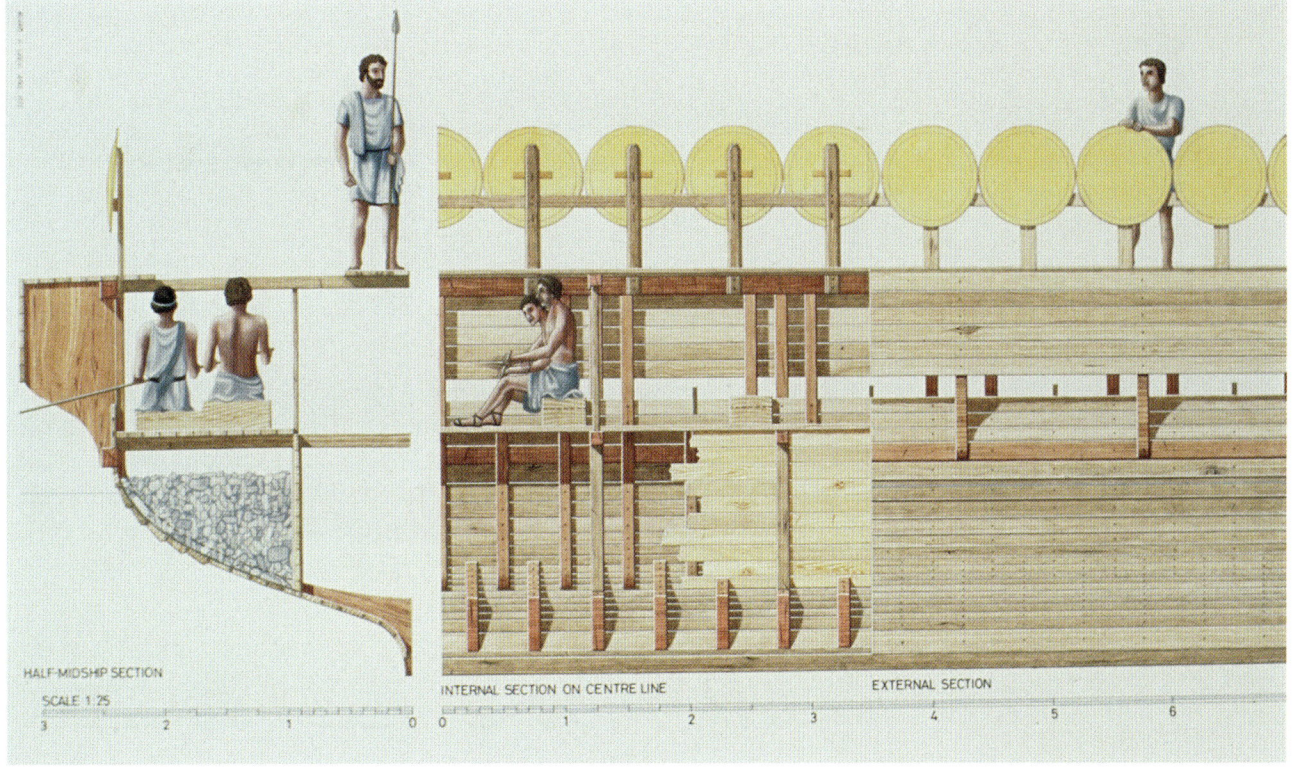

Pottery fragment discovered during an excavation of the Acropolis in Athens. It depicts a more advanced form of the bireme with rowers afforded better protection from missiles. Late Geometric II, c. 700 BC.

© Lucien Basch, *Le Musée imaginaire de la marine antique*

This fragment was excavated from the Kerameikos cemetery and dates from the Late Geometric I, c. 760-735 BC.

© Lucien Basch, *Le Musée imaginaire de la marine antique*

An Athenian black-figure *kylis* attributed to Nikosthenes. Although no oars are shown, this vase painting probably depicts a bireme, the lower oarsmen rowing through half-ports below the gunwale, the upper over the gunwale. The distortion at the bow is caused by the curvature of the vase. Late Archaic, c. 530-510 BC.

© Ink drawing by Michael Wedde from Pomey P., ed., *La Navigation dans l'Antiquité*

constituted the most important part of the ship and was used as an offensive weapon in battle. At its tip was the ram or rostrum, a pointed bronze head used to pierce the sides of enemy ships.

Propulsion was a more complicated affair for these vessels, as it was vital during battle to be able to manoeuvre and change course quickly in order to strike the enemy with the rostrum and at the same time avoid being hit by opposing ships. For this reason, the deck had two masts: the centre mast carried the mainsail and the other, in the prow, carried a small sail which made it possible to steer the ship even in crosswinds.

Although warships changed considerably over the centuries, Greek and Roman writers generally attribute the invention of their vessels to the Phoenicians. In the time of the early Phoenicians, warships had only one line of rowers. Around 30m long and 5m wide, these penteconters (meaning '50-oared') had platforms on either side of the hull from which soldiers could easily jump on to enemy ships.

The late 8th century BC saw the development of biremes. These were galleys with two banks of oars. The upper bank rowed from the deck, while the oars of those in the lower row passed through openings in the hull. The two banks of rowers were staggered to avoid entangling their oars. An illustration of a Phoenician bireme was discovered on a fragment of pottery dating from 700 BC, excavated clandestinely from the Kerameikos cemetry in Athens (left). It clearly depicts the two tiers of staggered oarsmen.

Triremes with three banks of oars appeared in the 7th century BC. These ships, invented by the Phoenicians, were also used by the Greeks and Romans and became the standard warship of the 3rd century BC. The wreck of the Isola Lunga, a 3rd century BC Punic warship, discovered near the Aegates Islands off the coast of Sicily, was probably a vessel of this type.

Wooden model of a trireme.

© Hellenic Maritime Museum

The number of rowers continued to increase, with the appearance of quadriremes (which Alexander the Great reported seeing in Phoenicia in 332 BC) and quinqueremes. According to Aristotle, the Phoenicians can also be credited with the invention of the quadrireme in the 4th century BC. This galley had only one bank of oars, but each was manned by four rowers. The quinquereme, with five rowers per oar, appeared soon afterwards.

Trading vessels, known by the Greeks as *gauloï*, a word that suggests roundness, certainly possessed a very deep hull and were almost as wide as they were long. Heavy and slow, they were designed for seaworthiness.

They were propelled by sail rather than oars, the latter being used only when absolutely necessary. Aristotle likened the sight of these *gauloï* plying their oars to huge, tiny-winged insects struggling unsuccessfully to fly.

The mast was fixed in the centre of the hull and the sail was attached to a yard, at the ends of which hung two halyards used to manoeuvre it. Additional ropes hanging from the centre served to roll up the sails and secure them when they were not in use.

These ships had two steering oars on either side of the stern, which was rounded and ended in an ornamental fish tail or volute. The prow, also curvilinear, was decorated with a zoomorphic frieze (often a horse's or seahorse's head).

Master seafarers

The Cape Gelidonya wreck

George Bass

In 1958, a sponge diver told American journalist Peter Throckmorton about a wreck lying 26m deep off Cape Gelidonya in Turkey. The following year Throckmorton located the site and realised it was the oldest shipwreck ever found, dating back to the Bronze Age.

Believing that underwater excavations could be conducted like those on land, he asked the University of Pennsylvania to send a scientific expedition to excavate the wreck. The mission, which I directed, was groundbreaking in a number of respects: it was the first time an archaeologist had studied an underwater site *in situ*, without using professional divers as an intermediary, and the first time an ancient wreck was excavated in its entirety on the seabed.

The wreck was that of a merchant ship that had pierced its hull on a submerged outcrop of rock in around 1200 BC, while trying to sail westward between two small islands just off the Cape. The ship and its cargo of copper and bronze from Cyprus was Near Eastern, or early Phoenician, in origin. This surprised the archaeologists, for in 1960 most scholars of Antiquity believed that Phoenicians did not begin their famed seafaring until the 8th century BC, during the later Iron Age. It was thought that Mycenaean Greeks held a monopoly on maritime commerce in the Bronze Age.

One lump of ingots from Area G required nearly a month of chiselling to free it from the rocky seabed.

© INA

I. The Phoenicians

The excavation

The team, with Throckmorton and myself, had to work in difficult conditions. The current was strong, and the depth of the wreck limited the length of dives. Further, many artefacts were covered in thick deposits of a rock-hard marine growth, accumulated over centuries, which prevented them from being identified underwater.

Using air-filled balloons and winches, the archaeologists brought huge

Because of the fragile wood remnants beneath the Area G ingots, they were removed carefully from the site and taken to the surface with the aid of an air-filled balloon.

© INA

lumps of artefact-filled concretions up to the two Turkish sponge-fishing boats from which they dived. Only at the surface were the artefacts cut loose from the concretions. The team then discovered a cargo of copper ingots and broken bronze tools, as well as evidence that the cargo was accompanied by a bronzesmith.

The seafaring bronzesmiths

The hull of the ship was for the most part destroyed, as it lay unprotected by sediment. Enough fragments of planking were preserved, however, to show that they had been held together by mortise-and-tenon joints like those in later Greek and Roman ships. The style of the tools and pottery showed that the wreck dates from around 1200 BC, a date confirmed by carbon 14 in brushwood laid under the cargo as a cushion.

The cargo largely consisted of bronze-making equipment. Thirty-four copper and several tin ingots were found (bronze is an alloy of copper and tin), as well as ingots of raw bronze, which were probably to be cast into tools. The copper ingots were cast in the shape of an ox-hide. This was simply to make them easier to handle and carry, and not, as was sometimes thought, because an ingot was of the same value as a cow.

Archaeologists discovered dozens of broken bronze tools such as scrap-axes, adzes, knives and a spade – all destined to be melted and cast into new bronze. A smith's tools were also found onboard, including a small anvil, hammers, a whetstone, stones to polish metals and a bronze block pierced with holes to make metal thread. These tools suggest that a smith sailed on the ship.

A Cypriot or Canaanite ship?

The copper ingots and scrap bronze all originated in Cyprus, but does that mean the ship was Cypriot in origin? A study of the personal possessions of the crew suggests that they were Canaanites – the early Phoenicians who settled in the area around modern Syria and Palestine.

The ship's only lamp and a pair of stone mortars were made in Syria, as were four scarabs and a cylindrical merchant's seal of the kind used by Near Eastern merchants to affix their signatures to clay tablets. The merchant on the Cape Gelidonya ship also carried nearly 60 graduated stone weights of Near Eastern origin, including Egyptian *qedets*, and Syrian and Canaanite *nesefs* and shekels.

In 1994, more than 30 years after the original excavation, diving archaeologists returned to the site and discovered nearly 100m away from the wreck the ship's stone anchor, of Near Eastern type.

The mariners onboard the ship must therefore have done business with Cypriots, but they themselves came from the area later called Phoenicia.

I. The Phoenicians

These three scarabs and the scarab-shaped plaque (inscribed on both sides), on the right, seem to have been manufactured on the Syro-Palestinian coast rather than in Egypt.

© INA

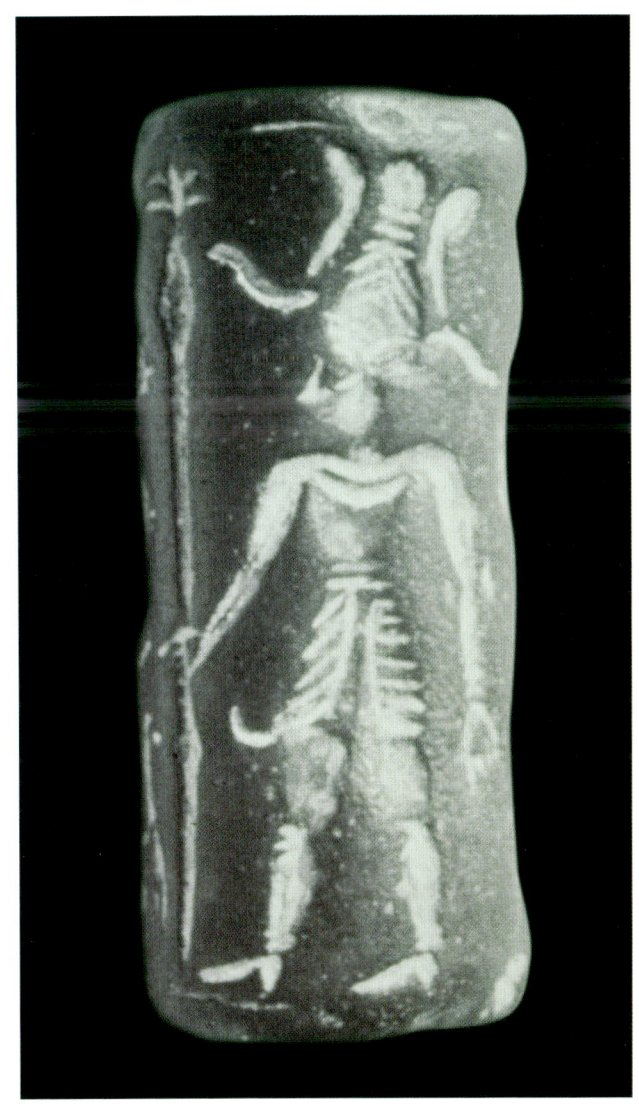

The merchant's cylindrical seal, found in the 'living quarters', is Syrian in origin.

© INA

Stone hammers shown alongside various bronze tools. All handles are modern.

© INA

Master seafarers

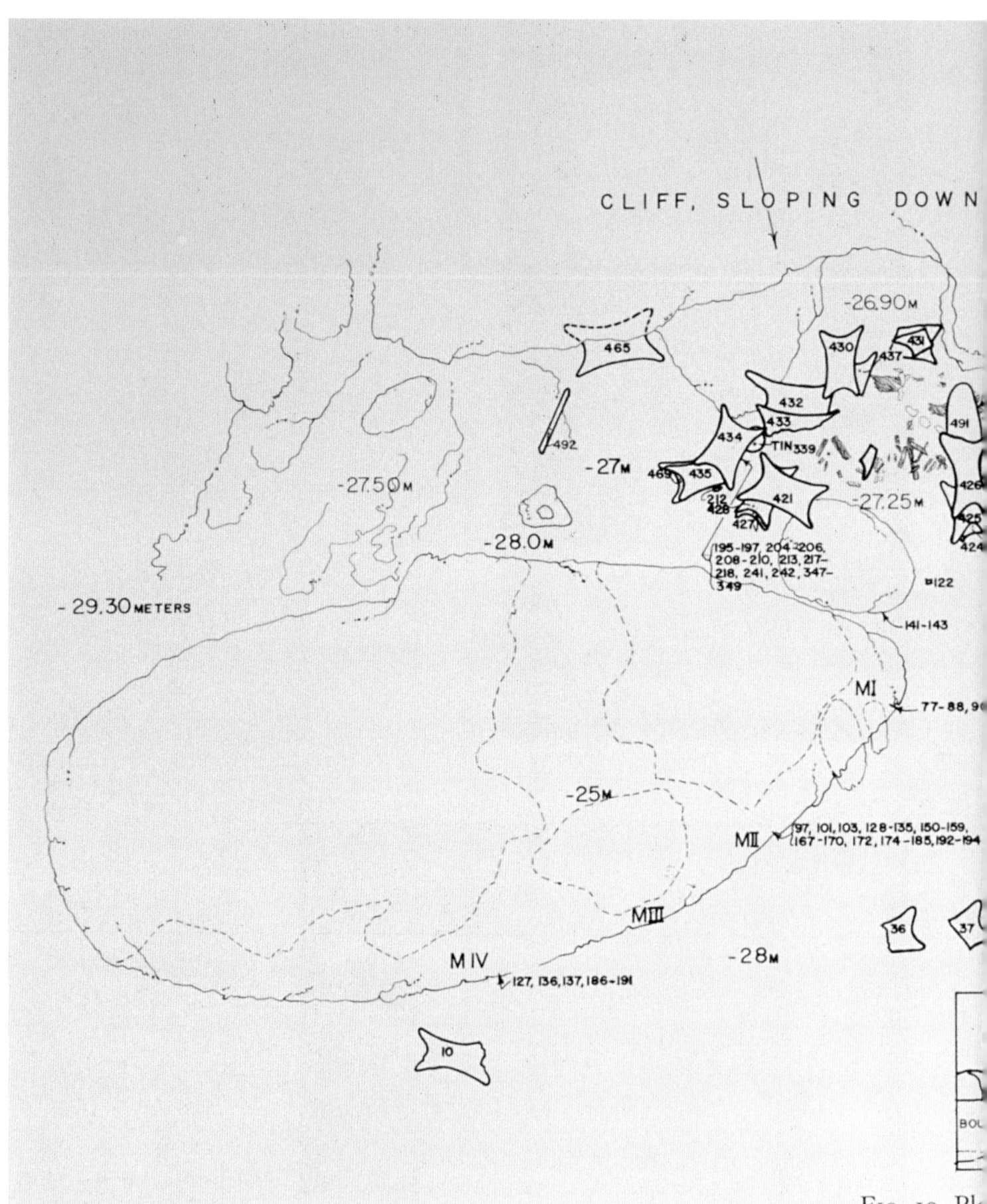

Map of the Cape Gelidonya site. © INA

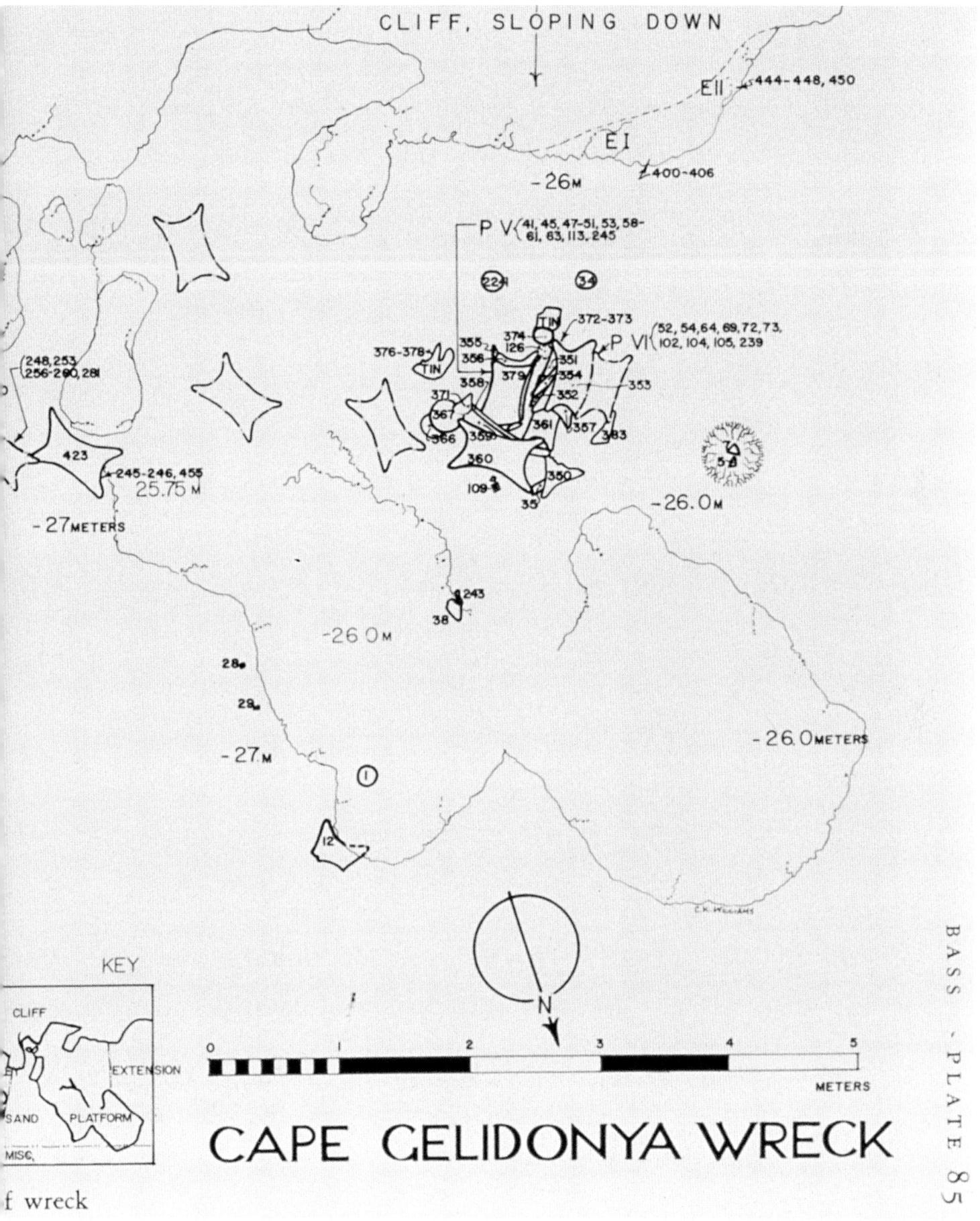

Cape Gelidonya: personal comment
George Bass

I believe that I was fated to go to Cape Gelidonya. Although I never dreamed that I would dive myself, I had read all the books on diving I could find from the time I was a small boy, even before Jacques-Yves Cousteau and Émile Gagnan had popularised diving by developing scuba equipment in the 1940s. So when my professor, Rodney Young, asked me in 1959 if I would learn to dive to excavate a Bronze Age shipwreck in Turkey, I accepted without hesitation and began a diving course.

The decision to return to Turkey was also easy for me, for it was a country I had first visited as a 20-year-old backpacker in 1953, and a country to which I returned in 1957 as a student assistant to Professor Young at his excavation of Gordion, the fabled city of King Midas. I was called on active duty in the US Army that year and sent to Korea, where I ended up as the only American officer commanding a unit inside the Turkish Brigade. Lastly, I already held a master's degree in Near Eastern archaeology, but was working on a doctorate in Classical archaeology, with a special interest in the Bronze Age Aegean.

Without this possibly unique academic background, I doubt that I would have recognised the historical significance of the Cape Gelidonya shipwreck. If I had been unfamiliar with Near Eastern archaeology, as are most Classical archaeologists, I surely would have assumed that the wreck was of a Bronze Age Greek, or Mycenaean, ship.

Indeed, all the Classical archaeologists who reviewed my publication of the site in 1967 said that I was wrong about the ship's Near Eastern origin. All of these scholars still accepted the prevailing view that Greeks held a monopoly on seafaring in the eastern Mediterranean during the Bronze Age.

The theory of Mycenaean dominance of the sea was based on the spread of Mycenaean pottery throughout the Near East, whereas little Near Eastern pottery is found on archaeological sites in Greece. It seemed to me that there was a flaw in this theory. I pointed out that Mycenaean pottery was not given out gratis, that something of equal value had to have been coming to Greece from the Near East in return. But what could this have been?

Return visits to the site in the late 1980s, nearly 30 years after the original excavation, located two well preserved Mycenaean III B stirrup jars about 50m from the main area of wreckage.
© INA

It left no trace in the archaeological record. I suggested that the goods coming to Greece from the Near East were raw materials such as copper, tin, gold, and ivory, all of which would have been manufactured into typically Mycenaean products soon after arriving at Greek ports, leaving no trace of their Near Eastern origins.

More than 20 years later, the excavation of the Bronze Age shipwreck at Uluburun, Turkey, with its tons of raw copper, tin, ivory, wood, resin, glass, and more, proved me right.

How many graduate students of archaeology in 1959 owned as many books on diving as on archaeology? How many had already worked in Turkey and longed to return? And how many had studied Near Eastern and pre-Classical Greek archaeology equally? Surely I just chanced to be the right person at the right time when I approached my professor.

Above: Archaeologists diving from two sponge boats.

© INA

Left: Peter Dorrell, George Bass, Peter Throckmorton and Honor Frost (from left to right) work on the site map.

© INA

Terracotta head of the Punic goddess Tanit.

© Roger Wood/CORBIS

The Tanit and Elissa wrecks

During a mission in the summer of 1997, the highly advanced sonar of an American nuclear submarine detected three wreck sites off the coast near Ashkelon, in Israel. This discovery aroused great interest among archaeologists, who believed that two of the wrecks could date from the Iron Age and therefore deserved to be fully investigated.

An expedition was organised by the IFE (Institute for Exploration) in 1999. The team was made up of archaeologists from the Leon Levy Expedition to Ashkelon, headed by Lawrence E. Stager, a Harvard University professor. Oceanographers and engineers from the Woods Hole Oceanographic Institution, the Massachusetts Institute of Technology and John Hopkins University also assisted the expedition leader, Dr Robert Ballard.

The Tanit wreck, named in honour of the goddess Tanit, the Iron Age guardian of Phoenician sailors, and the Elissa wreck, named after a Tyrian princess, the sister of Pygmalion, are the oldest wrecks ever discovered in deep water, at a depth of 400m. Both were Phoenician merchant ships dating from the 8th century BC.

Archaeologists involved in the excavation worked aboard the *Northern Horizon*, a converted British trawler equipped with two very sophisticated submarines, the *Jason* and the *Medea*, both of which were equipped with sonar and the latest high-tech photographic equipment. They also used the very powerful DSL-120, a 120kHz sidescan sonar. This extremely advanced technology, combined with painstaking work by scientists, made it possible for the team to pinpoint the two wrecks' exact location.

They began by sending the two submarines to carry out a detailed hydrographic survey of the sites. Then they systematically photographed both wrecks and collated the series of pictures to form a photomosaic of the entire archaeological site. This photomosaic image – composed of smaller pictures taken using powerful spotlights – was essential to the archaeologists' work, as there was insufficient underwater light for the scientific study of a large surface area.

However, although the image offered scientists a clearer view of the wreck, it did not allow them to extract accurate data. They therefore undertook a bathymetric survey of the site. This imaging system, combined with various charts of the seabed produced by sonar scans, provided a comprehensive picture of the ships and their cargoes of amphorae, and a better idea of which artefacts to remove. This proved to be a time-consuming, painstaking task.

The next stage involved bringing to the surface some of these artefacts that were regarded as useful for determining the ships' ages and origins. This was not an easy task. Robots armed with articulated pincers had to be used to delicately extract the selected artefacts without disturbing the site. Each artefact removed was then placed in a net and brought to the surface using a hoist. Their exact location was carefully recorded on the photomosaic and the excavation map.

I. The Phoenicians

Three jugs with mushroom-shaped brims.
© Gianni Dagli Orti/CORBIS

Phoenician shipwrecks from the deep sea: Tanit and Elissa

Lawrence E. Stager

Some time between 750 and 700 BC a fleet of Phoenician ships was sailing about 33 nautical miles offshore – on an east-west line connecting the ancient seaport of Ashkelon with the delta of Egypt, and further west with Carthage – when gusts of wind from the Sinai coast caught the sailors by surprise.

The abrupt shift in Mediterranean winds, firstly from the northeast, then to the southeasterly 'sirocco' wind, created a storm that swamped two of these modest-sized merchantmen. They foundered and plunged upright into the soft, clayey bottom of the Mediterranean some 400m below the surface, in waters too deep to be explored by usual underwater archaeological techniques.

There these two shipwrecks lay, about 2km apart, largely undisturbed

Table showing the evolution of shapes in Phoenician pottery

I. The Phoenicians

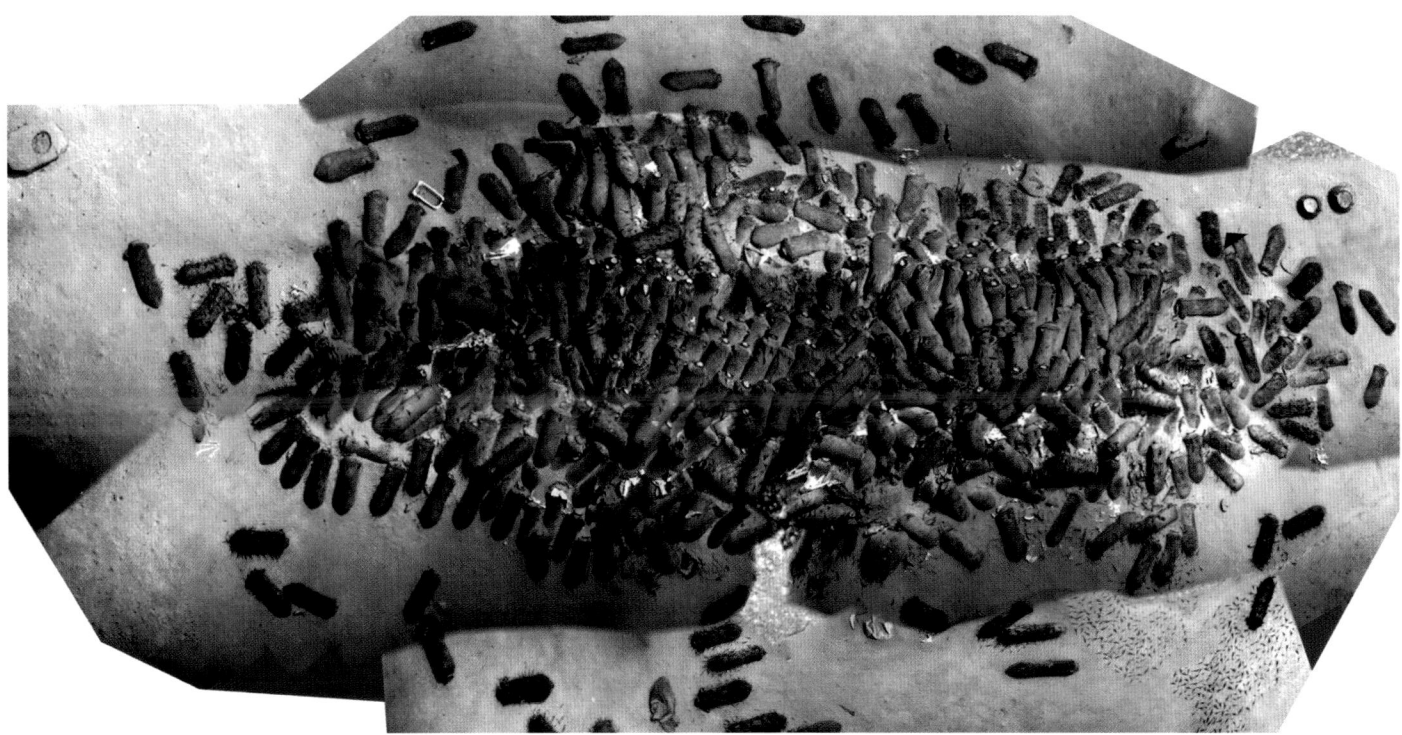

Photomosaic of the Tanit, a wreck from c. 750 BC. Tanit, protector of Phoenician seafarers, was the Iron Age successor to the Canaanite god Astarte.

© Institute For Exploration, Woods Hole Oceanographic Institution, and the Leon Levy expedition to Ashkelon

and undetected, until the US Navy's nuclear research submarine, the NR-1, searching for a lost Israeli submarine, identified three wrecks in 1997. Videotapes of two of these wrecks were shown to Dr Robert Ballard, founder and director of the IFE, who, in turn, invited me to view them. Although the videos were quite blurred and hazy, I thought that at least one of the wreck sites looked ancient, perhaps as early as the Iron Age. With the hope of finding the oldest deep-sea shipwrecks, we decided to launch an expedition to survey, plan, and photograph the wrecks in 1999.

The size of the ships

Fairly soon after Tanit and Elissa had sunk and plunged into the muddy seabed up to their decks, scouring took place along the contours of their wooden hulls, exposing hundreds of amphorae stacked in tiers 1.5m-2m deep.

The contours of their cargoes retain the shape of a ship, outlining the forms of their long-vanished hulls, thus providing the ships' approximate dimensions.

Microbathymetry provided the most precise measurements of the two shipwrecks. In cargo size, Tanit measured 4.5m by 11.5m, Elissa, 5m by 12m. By extension this would give the two ships a length of about 14m to 14.5m from prow to stern and a beam width of about 5.5m to 6m.

The crew and their home port

The personal belongings of the crews of Tanit and Elissa consisted of cooking pots, with close parallels to those found in coastal Lebanon: a

Elissa (Shipwreck B) c. 750 BC. Elissa, Tyrian princess and sister of the Tyrian king Pum'yaton (better known as Pygmalion), fled from mainland Phoenicia to Cyprus taking with her a crew of Phoenicians. According to legend she went on to found Carthage.

© Institute For Exploration, Woods Hole Oceanographic Institution, and the Leon Levy expedition to Ashkelon

handmade bowl, which originated in Egypt; a *mortarium* from coastal Syria, for grinding condiments; a small one-quarter amphora for wine; a wine decanter with mushroom-shaped rim for libations; and a small portable incense stand.

The personal belongings of the crew always provide the best indication of a ship's origin or nationality. In this case both the cargo of amphorae and the crew's property suggest a Phoenician origin, and a date in the latter half of the 8th century BC. The single most telling artefact is the mushroom-lipped wine decanter. The mushroom-style rim, whether on jugs, juglets, or decanters, is the unmistakable 'signature' of the Phoenicians, wherever they sailed.

Cargoes

The most common artefacts by far aboard the two ships were amphorae. The empty jars weigh on average 6.7kg each; when filled with water or wine each amphora weighs on average 24.68kg. The amphora type is well known from land excavations in the Levant, being commonly found in sites occupied or destroyed by the Assyrians in the latter half of the 8th century BC, such as Megiddo III, Hazor VI-V, and Tyre III-II.

The centres of production for torpedo-shaped amphorae, such as were found aboard the wreck, were in Phoenicia. In the 8th century BC the most important Phoenician port was the island-city of Tyre and it is there that kiln-wasters of this very type of torpedo-shaped amphora were discovered.

The amphorae retrieved from the two shipwrecks had once been lined on the interior with resin, which tests determined was pine pitch. Tartaric acid was trapped in this pitch, indicating that the amphorae had once been filled with wine.

The amphorae themselves were remarkably similar in shape and size, each holding on average 17.8 litres of wine. The standardisation of containers is among the most exact prior to modern mass production and attests to the division of labour commonly associated with a large and wide-reaching market.

Destination

The intended destination of Tanit and Elissa is not known. One possibility is that they were headed toward Carthage. They sank about the time that Phoenician colonies were being founded in the central and western Mediterranean, Carthage being the most famous.

Excavations at both Carthage and contemporary colonies in Spain have yielded large quantities of torpedo-shaped amphorae, identical in type to those on our two shipwrecks and imported from the Levant. The other, and in my opinion, the more likely destination of this large cargo of wine was Egypt. At least one item of the crew's personal pottery – the round-bottomed bowl – came from Egypt.

More helpful in determining the destination of the principal cargo of 11 tonnes of wine on each ship is our knowledge of the wine trade between Phoenicia and Egypt in the Persian period. In a list of commodities imported into Egypt from Ionia and Phoenicia in 475 BC, wine was the primary cargo. We also know that several Phoenician ships reached Egypt during the last three months of that year. In addition to a primary cargo of wine, these ships carried metal ingots of copper, iron and tin. Also onboard were supplies of timber, most probably cedars from Lebanon, bundles of wool, and potter's clay.

Disaster on a deep-sea route

Do Tanit and Elissa, so far from shore and on a line between the north Sinai coast and the Egyptian delta, mark a trade route used by the Phoenicians in the 8th century BC? The usual but unproven notion is that ancient seafarers followed the prevailing winds as they sailed in a counter-clockwise circuit around the Mediterranean.

The Ashkelon shipwrecks had not capsized, hurling their cargoes of amphorae and anchors overboard. Rather they settled quietly to the bottom on an even keel, plunging upright but deep into the soft clay sediments of the sea floor. This suggests that the ships had been swamped by a great storm wave while tacking before the wind, most likely during one of the fierce desert storms so common along this part of the north Sinai coast.

Texts such as Ezekiel 27 reveal that Phoenician seafarers took a direct route across the 'deep sea' (in Hebrew, *mayim rabbim*) by about 600 BC. However, the location of our Phoenician shipwrecks seems to indicate that the Phoenicians were sailing directly across the Mediterranean as much as 250 years before that.

If this was a common route, there may be a myriad of these ships waiting to be discovered in the 'deep sea', and today we have the technology available to discover these lost ships, and thereby chart their ancient routes.

The team

The overall project was directed by Dr Robert Ballard of the IFE, with Professor Lawrence E. Stager of Harvard University in charge of the archaeological team. The work was sponsored by the Office of Naval Research, the National Geographic Society and by Leon Levy and Shelby White.

The Mazarron 1 excavation. Divers have laid out the grid system across the remains of the hull. Plastic sacks lie nearby for raising artefacts.

© Museo Nacional de Arqueologia Maritima, Cartagena.
Photo: P. Ortiz

Mazarron 1 and 2

The best archaeology often happens quite by chance, for example when ruins are unearthed in the course of construction work on modern building sites. So it was in September 1994, when a wreck was discovered during the building of a marina on the Playa de la Isla, in the town of Mazarron in southern Spain. Five years later, CENIAS (the Spanish National Centre for Underwater Archaeological Research), with the support of the Spanish authorities, embarked on a two-year excavation. Their mission was christened the 'Barco Fenicio' (Phoenician ship) project and involved 13 full-time members led by Dr Iván Negueruela. The multidisciplinary group included archaeologists, curators and photographers, assisted from time to time by Spanish and European researchers.

Little could be deduced about the ship or the circumstances surrounding its loss, but its cargo proved to be a veritable treasure trove. Although the physical and chemical action of the seawater over a 2000-year period could easily have completely destroyed the boat's wooden structure, part of the wreck survived due to the protective layer of sand which covered it.

A small ship from the 7th century BC

The first stage of the excavation was to carry out a systematic survey of the site over an area of 72,000m^2, without disturbing what was left of the ship. Researchers embarked on a detailed topographical analysis of the site, after which archaeologists began their investigation of the ship and its cargo. Some artefacts were removed and sent to the National Museum of Underwater Archaeology in Cartagena, where they were chemically treated to prepare them for more detailed analysis and preservation.

The ship measured 5.5m in length and was 1.3m wide, whereas initial estimates had put its size at 8m long and 2m wide. Its hull, buried under a thin layer of sand, was in an excellent state of preservation. A few keel timbers had survived, as well as some planking. The keel fragments were 4m long and nine wooden planks were attached to the hull by mortise-and-tenon joints, which were widely used in ancient times. On both sides of the wreck, inside and out, archaeologists found resin, which was undoubtedly used to make the ship watertight. Several pieces of petrified rope were also discovered.

By making underwater casts of the ship's structure and the excavated fragments, archaeologists were able to reconstruct 40% of the ship. This reconstruction is currently on display at the National Museum of Underwater Archaeology, in Cartagena.

An extremely varied cargo

The ship was transporting a variety of pottery and metal objects. No fewer than 7,500 artefacts were uncovered during the excavation. The majority of these were practical everyday items that navigators would have used during their voyage: flat and round-bottomed plates, pots and pans. Archaeologists also discovered urns, baskets, a cargo of amphorae, mortars, religious objects and carafes. It didn't take long to locate these pieces of pottery beneath the wood of the boat, covered by 4cm to 5cm of sand.

Nearly three-quarters of them were manufactured in Phoenicia. In addition to these artefacts, the team also found a finely crafted silver scarab ring and a bronze spear.

All that remained was to accurately date the ship from the artefacts that had been found. Seventy per cent of the material was estimated to have come from the second half of the 7th century BC, whereas the remaining 30% ranged in date from Antiquity to the present-day. The ship's structure and construction method were consistent with those from the first half of the 1st millennium BC. For more accurate dating, timber and seaweed samples were sent to Groningen University in Holland for laboratory analysis, which showed that the ship dated from 650-600 BC.

During the project, to everyone's surprise, another wreck was discovered, complete with its reasonably well preserved cargo. It was buried beneath the

Divers on the Mazarron excavation casting silicone moulds of the timbers.

© Museo Nacional de Arqueologia Maritima, Cartagena.
Photo: P. Ortiz

I. The Phoenicians

Freeing the anchor and its hawser, from the seafloor.

© Museo Nacional de Arqueologia Maritima, Cartagena.
Photo: P. Ortiz

sand at a depth of around 2m. The archaeologists did not want to begin work on this second wreck before they had a chance to establish the conditions necessary for a proper, dedicated excavation.

This required a budget of more than 1.2 million euros, most of which was used to build a 12m long, 7m wide shelter to house the entire ship and protect it from breaking up. This construction contained all the equipment needed to preserve the wreck, carry out the complicated task of restoring it and eliminate the salt which could destroy the timber as it dried out.

In January 2000, the ship's anchor, rudder and mast were brought to the surface. However, the wreck still lies on the sea floor and the project has been put on hold as the museum lacks the necessary space to house and preserve it.

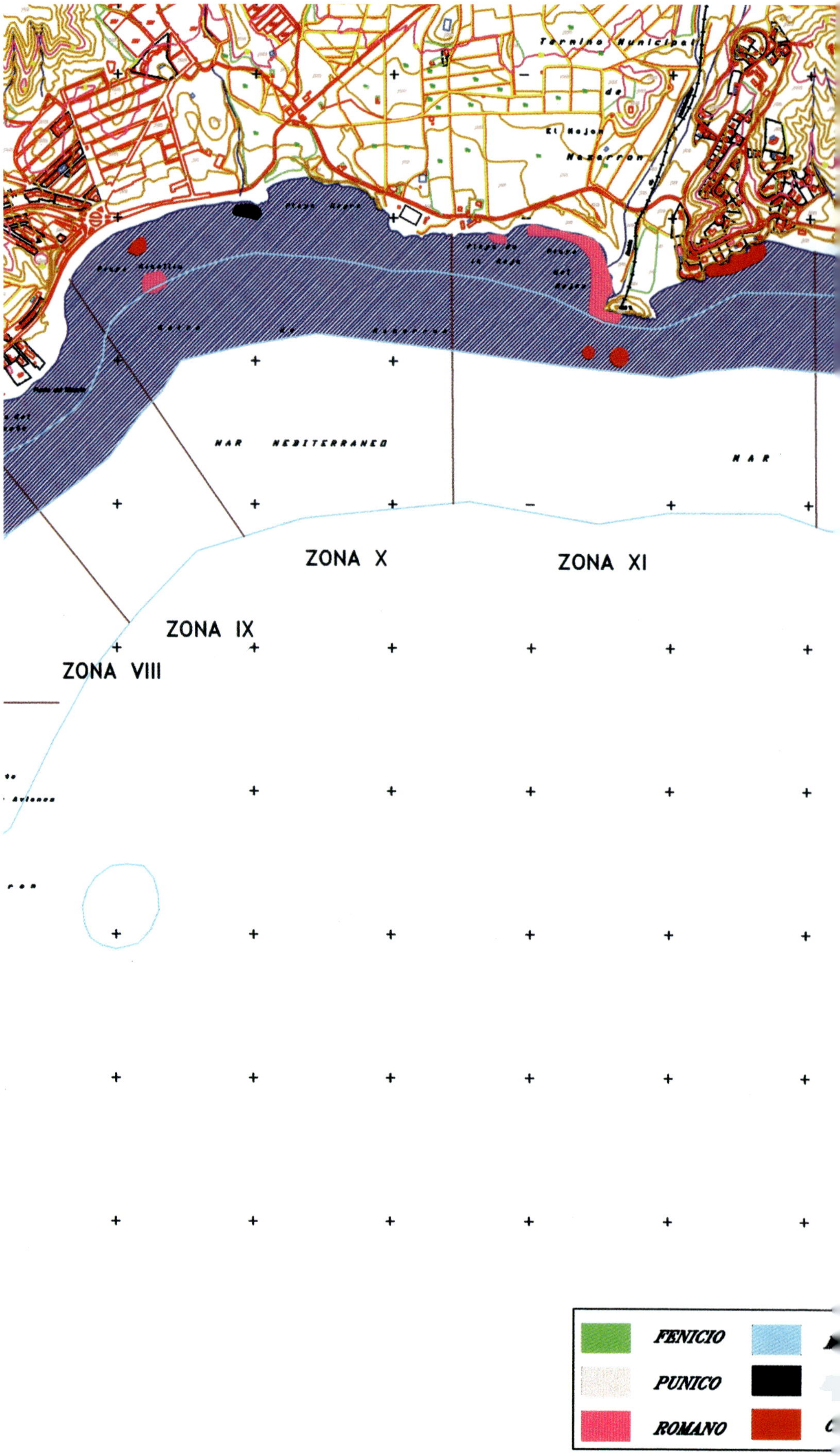

Master seafarers

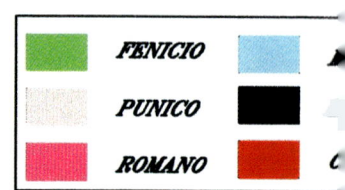

Partial view of the macrospatial survey near Mazarron 2, 6km² have been prospected.

© Museo Nacional de Arqueologia Maritima, Cartagena

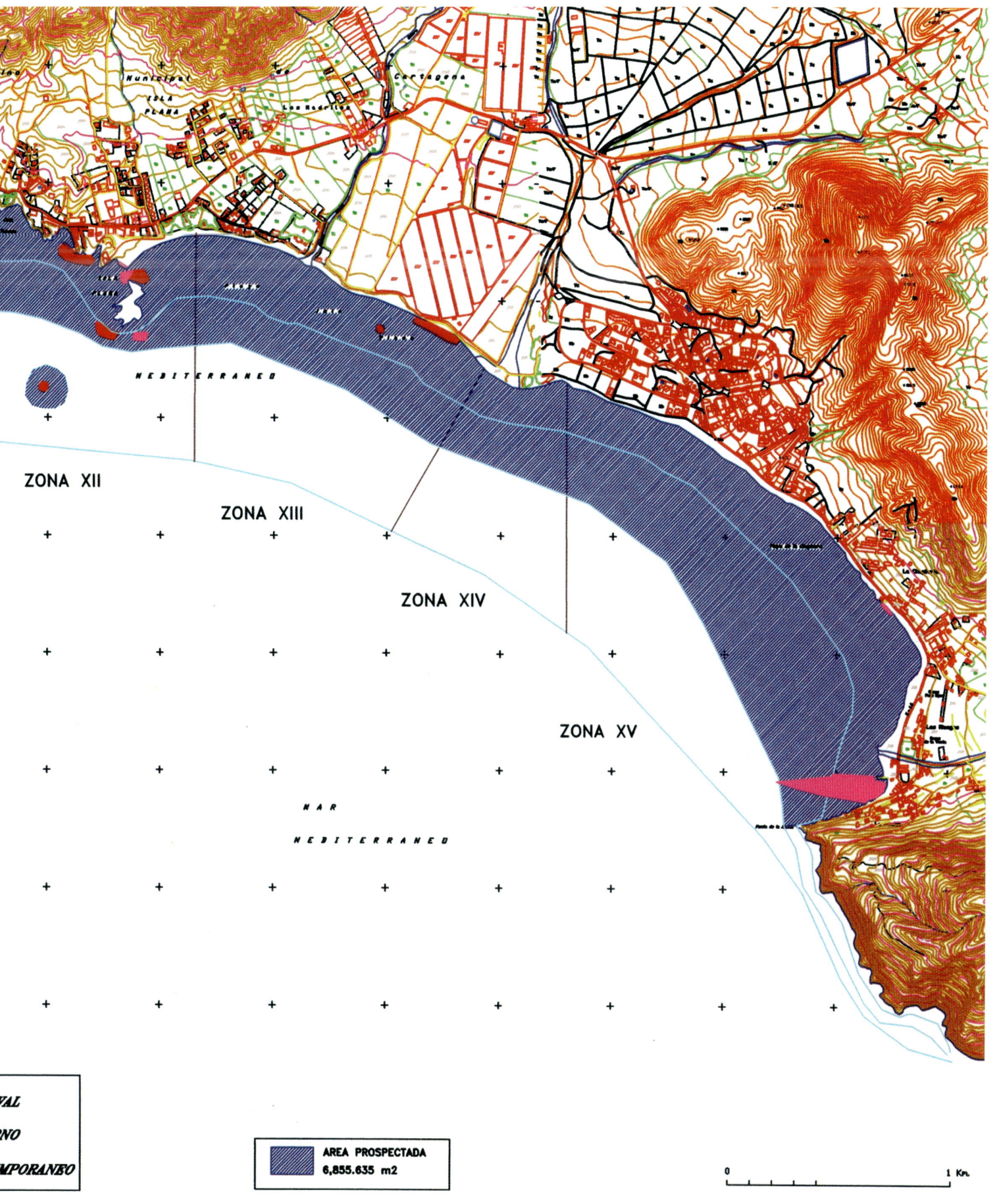

Mazarron 2

The Mazarron 2 wreck was discovered in 1994 not far from that of Mazarron 1 by the team of Dr Iván Negueruela, director of the National Museum of Underwater Archaeology in Cartagena.

The protective covering which shielded the Phoenician ship during the excavation.
© Museo Nacional de Arqueologia Maritima, Cartagena
Photo: P. Ortiz

It lay completely buried in sand at a depth of less than 2m. Construction of a marina in the 1980s caused a change in the ocean currents and altered the natural silting up of the site, which is how Mazarron 2 came to light.

The hull was complete and extremely well preserved. Archaeologists identified the mast housing from among the scattered parts of the keelson.

The whole cargo had been protected by a colony of underwater plants that had to be removed. Excavators discovered a common type of Phoenician amphora frequently found near the Malaga coast, rigging, a wooden-handled basket and two pieces of a granite grinding wheel.

It seems likely that all these finds were actually in use onboard the ship. Animal bones discovered on the site were also analysed and identified, showing that the crew had eaten goat, rabbit and chicken.

The remaining cargo was made up entirely of lead ingots. We know from ancient texts that a trade route existed along the coasts of southern Spain, mainly via Cadiz, and was used by the Phoenicians for transporting metals. The Mazarron 2 cargo is the first clear and tangible evidence that such a route existed.

The planking ribs were held together by mortise-and-tenon joints, and were attached to the central part of the hull by ligatures. The hull interior was coated with resin.

Precise measurements can be taken against the solid frame of the covering.
© Museo Nacional de Arqueologia Maritima, Cartagena.
Photo: P. Ortiz

The ship's anchor, which was made of lead and wood, was found near the bow, together with the rope that once held it.

The construction methods, which are characteristic of Phoenician maritime engineering, the cargo of lead ingots and the Phoenician amphorae leave no doubt as to the ship's origin. However, it is difficult to say with certainty which route it was following, where it had come from and where it was headed.

I. The Phoenicians

Above: The protective caisson, assembled on the seabed to shield Mazarron 2.

Below: The ship during the first phase of excavation. The anchor is visible to the left.

© Museo Nacional de Arqueologia Maritima, Cartagena.
Photos: P. Ortiz

The protective covering

In order to protect wrecks from further damage by nature or human hands, archaeologists normally rebury them in sand once the excavations have been completed. This is a tedious process because the sand has to be removed again for each new campaign.

The Spanish team from Cartagena developed and constructed a highly effective protective covering which is much less cumbersome. This technique can be used for any small or medium-sized wreck as long as its height does not exceed a few metres – in other words most of the Phoenician, Greek and Roman ships scattered around the Mediterranean sea floor.

The structure is made of metal and is fixed to the seabed by means of several steel uprights. It is made up of 1m^2 hinged plates, which are linked together and can be individually opened and closed.

During an excavation, only the plates above the sections being investigated are open. The other plates remain

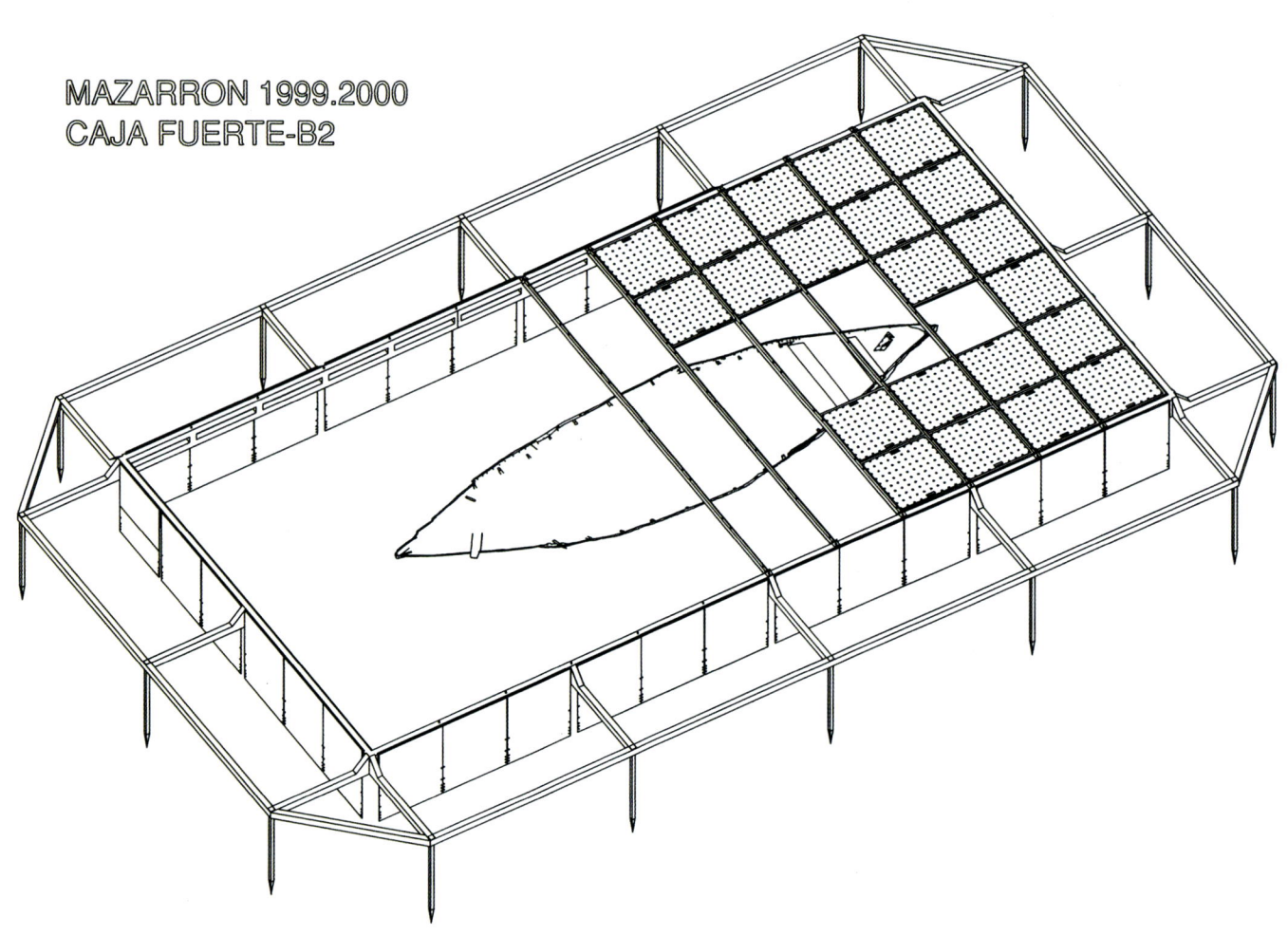

The protective covering of Mazarron 2, designed by the MNAM to protect the wreck from the elements and the work of the divers during the excavation.

© Museo Nacional de Arqueologia Maritima, Cartegena

I. The Phoenicians

The wreck and its cargo photographed from the prow.
© Museo Nacional de Arqueologia Maritima, Cartagena.
Photo: P. Ortiz

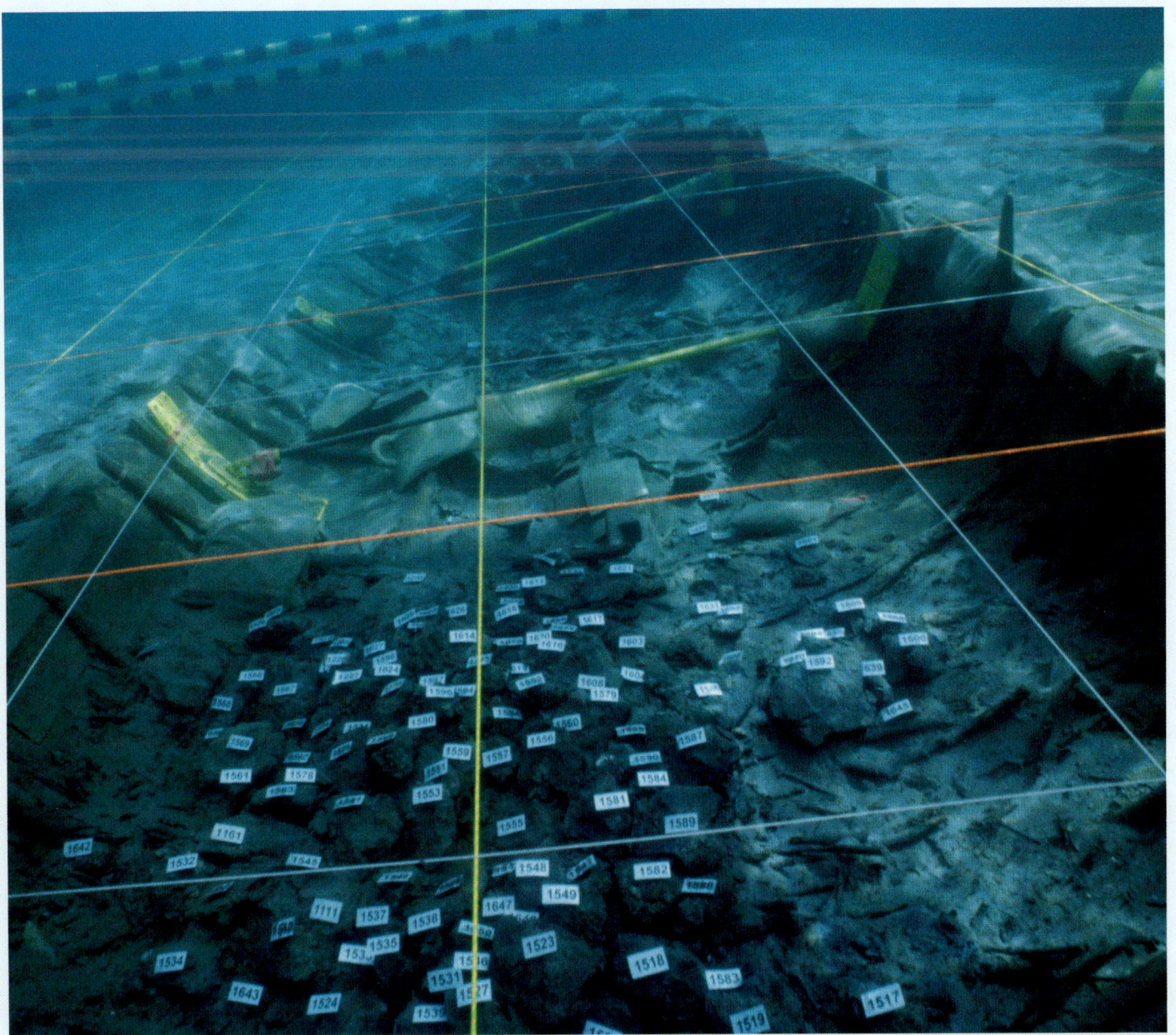

closed to protect the remains. This system enables excavators to move about freely and work on specific areas without running the risk of damaging the rest of the wreck. It also provides a useful place for them to store the instruments needed to complete their tasks.

At the end of a day's work, the cover is completely closed up. Should excavations be interrupted for a period of several months or more, the cover is camouflaged with a tumulus of sand and stones. This leaves the wreck totally protected not only from the forces of nature but also from unscrupulous amateur archaeologists or even worse, from organised looters.

The Ma'agan Mikhael wreck

The site where wreck was discovered, near the Ma'agan Mikhael kibbutz on the Israeli coast, was used as a training area for divers from the Archaeological Undersea Exploration Society of Israel. However, no remains had ever been found off this sandy coast until a member of the kibbutz came across some pieces of wood, a pile of large stones and pottery shards, while diving in shallow water in September 1985. The section of wood protruding from the sand was buried much deeper than he was able to reach with his bare hands. He realised that this pile of debris might well conceal something of great interest and value, as the stones were not typical of the region and the shards appeared ancient.

Dr Elisha Linder, professor of maritime studies at the Institute of Maritime Archaeology at the University of Haifa was quickly notified and realised as soon as he saw the wreck that this was an amazing discovery – a merchant ship dating from about 400 BC with the hull still intact. With the help of a team of archaeologists and engineers from the Recanati Institute of Maritime Studies at the University of Haifa and other experts, Dr Linder decided to excavate. The excavation took place in three phases between 1988 and 1989.

The treasures that had been discovered could not be left where they lay, so close to land and in shallow waters, especially the wreck itself which was so well preserved. Extricating such an ancient and fragile ship is no easy task, but these archaeologists rose to the challenge, dismantling the boat's hull underwater and transferring it to the conservation laboratory at Haifa University.

After a seven-year process of conservation by immersion in polyethylene glycol, the boat was finally reconstructed under the supervision of Yaacov Kahanov, and moved to a museum adjacent to the University of Haifa, the Edith and Reuven Hecht Archaeological Museum – renamed the Ma'agan Mikhael Museum in June 1999. Kahanov is now curator of the museum, which is used as a laboratory for scientific, archaeological and historical research as well as being open to the general public.

The wooden anchor of the Ma'agan Mikhael ship. This was raised to the surface.

© Itamar Grinberg

Divers holding a section of the hull.

© Itamar Grinberg

The ship and the finds

Yaacov Kahanov

The Ma'agan Mikhael ship, discovered in 1985 off the Mediterranean coast of Israel, 35km south of Haifa in shallow water, was buried under a layer of sand about 1.5m deep. The ship was discovered by Ami Eshel, a member of Kibbutz Ma'agan Mikhael. While diving along the coast he noticed a pile of unusual stones mixed with ceramics and wood. He alerted the authorities, and the excavation and research of the ship began.

The maximum length of the preserved portion of the hull was 11.15m, and its maximum breadth was 3.11m. The ship was dated, using carbon 14 analysis and ceramic evaluations, to the end of the 5th century BC.

The ship carried about 13 tonnes of stones and rocks of non-local types.

Most of the load was made up of blue schist, which upon analysis seemed to come from the Greek island of Euboea (Evvia). Other stones among those found were magmatic, from the small delta of the Kouris river, southern Cyprus.

The 70 ceramic items retrieved include a *pithos*, basket-handle jars, oil lamps, small jugs, *mortaria* (shallow bowls for food preparation), other bowls, and a cooking pot. Most of the ceramics can be attributed to Cyprus, although some were identified as having their origin in eastern Greece.

Food remnants were also found, as well as ropes, lead fishing weights, carpenter's tools and a single-armed wooden anchor. The anchor was found close to the ship's bow, with both the main line and trip rope still attached.

The entire lower part of the hull remained intact up to the third strake, including the false keel, keel, stem and sternpost. Portions of 12 strakes up to the second wale survived on the starboard side. Also surviving were two knees, 14 frames, the mast step, and several additional internal components.

No barnacles or other bio-fouling traces were found and only limited teredo damage was identified on the uppermost parts of some timbers. Bark still adhered to some of the interior parts. The exterior parts seemed to have just come out of the shipyard, with sharp corners and edges and no sign of abrasion. This was also the case with the anchor. Adze, saw and chisel marks were clearly visible, and wood shavings remained inside the ship. All of which suggest that the ship had made very few voyages. She was found with her bow pointing perpendicular to the shore, apparently having been sailing under control when she was wrecked.

The ship was carvel-built by the 'shell-first' method, with the strakes connected by means of closely spaced mortise-and-tenon joints fastened by tapered pegs. In addition to these joints, the bow and the stern assemblies of the ship were sewn. The full frames were made of specially selected, naturally curving crotch–timber floors and futtocks, hook-scarfed along the same plane. The widely spaced frames were attached to the hull by copper nails that were hammered in from the outside of the planks through the frames and then double-clenched on the inner frame surfaces.

Comparison with several similar shipwrecks found in the Mediterranean has not resolved the question of the ship's origin, or ports of call on her last passage, although some inferences regarding her Greek construction tradition have been made. The keel, end posts, planks, frames and other internal components were made of pine, while the tenons, tapered pegs, false keel, and anchor were of oak.

After the contents had been retrieved, the hull was dismantled underwater and the pieces were transferred to the conservation laboratory at the University of Haifa.

The first conservation phase was desalination, which lasted two years. This was followed by a five-year conservation process in polyethylene glycol (PEG 4000). After a year of seasoning the pieces were transferred to a purpose-built museum. Over the next three years the ship was reassembled, a process which was combined with a thorough research study of the hull construction details. Finally, the ship has been reassembled and is on exhibition in the university museum.

The excavation was undertaken by Elisha Linder, a prominent Israeli underwater archaeologist who established the Department of Maritime Civilizations and the Recanati Institute for Maritime Studies at the University of Haifa in 1972. Financial support was provided by Lord Jacobs and the University of Haifa, the field director of the three seasons of excavations was Jay Rosloff and the ship was conserved, reassembled and studied by myself.

Planks from the Ma'agan Mikhael wreck.

© Itamar Grinberg

Ma'agan Mikhael: personal comment

Yaacov Kahanov

The Ma'agan Mikhael shipwreck was a fascinating source of information for archaeologists, like myself, who were lucky enough to be a part of the study, which spanned half a generation.

Firstly, the method of research itself was very interesting, as over the course of the study several of the preliminary hypotheses needed to be revised. This shows scientific research at its most honest, with young students encouraged to challenge existing theories.

Another notable aspect of the methodology was the reassembly of the boat, which to an outsider looks like an enormous jigsaw puzzle comprised of many similar-looking dark, hard pieces of wood. Identifying the different components and establishing their original location on the boat can be achieved by examining staining patterns, attachment features, and how the various joints fit together. An in-depth study of the ship soon familiarises the researcher with the different sections and reassembling them is then a mere technical matter. There was no margin for error, however. If at any stage components had not been assembled correctly, it became apparent later on, and the incorrectly assembled parts had to be redone.

In fact, we found that it was almost as if the ship were instructing us how properly to reconstruct her. It is an incredible feeling when the ancient dark timbers begin to communicate to you as you study them.

Yet while the research continued, many technical questions remained unanswered. Taking thousands of measurements, recording the ship's features, evaluating statistics and interpreting, served only to raise more questions about the vessel, rather than solving them. Important technical problems were eventually solved not by technical calculations, but through a very human analysis of the evidence.

More than a dozen students participated in the reassembly of the ship's hull and each was assigned a specific research topic. Having hands-on access to the construction secrets of ancient shipwrights is an opportunity seldom granted to nautical archaeology students. Combined with exposure to such a demanding scientific approach, it was a unique educational experience for the young archaeologists.

Above: Initial phase of reconstruction work on the surface.

Opposite: Some time later and the reconstruction is more complete.

© Itamar Grinberg

I. The Phoenicians

Master seafarers

The Melkarth wreck

In 1998, Greg Stemm, co-founder and director of operations at Odyssey Marine Exploration Inc., set off in search of an English warship, the *HMS Sussex*, lost at sea more than 300 years earlier. The vessel was loaded with gold and silver coins with an estimated value of US$500 million. However, Stemm's search revealed something else.

On 17 September, at a depth of more than 800m, he discovered an ancient ship containing hundreds of Carthaginian amphorae. This Punic or Phoenician ship could be dated to between the 5th and 3rd centuries BC. During the expedition, Stemm and his team used a 30m long boat equipped with sidescan sonar. Each time a target was detected, the team checked and analysed its archaeological importance by sending down an ROV (Remotely operated vehicle) fitted with powerful spotlights and photographic equipment.

The type of amphorae discovered was extremely rare. Their colour ranged from red to brown, they were 1m high and their weight was equally distributed between their belly and neck (see diagram below). Similar amphorae, typically Carthaginian and dating from 450 BC, have been found in Morocco, Spain and Greece – all of which were Phoenician trading destinations.

The question of whether the ship came from Carthage or Phoenicia cannot therefore be answered by the amphorae alone. It is quite possible that the eastern Phoenicians loaded them when they docked at Carthage.

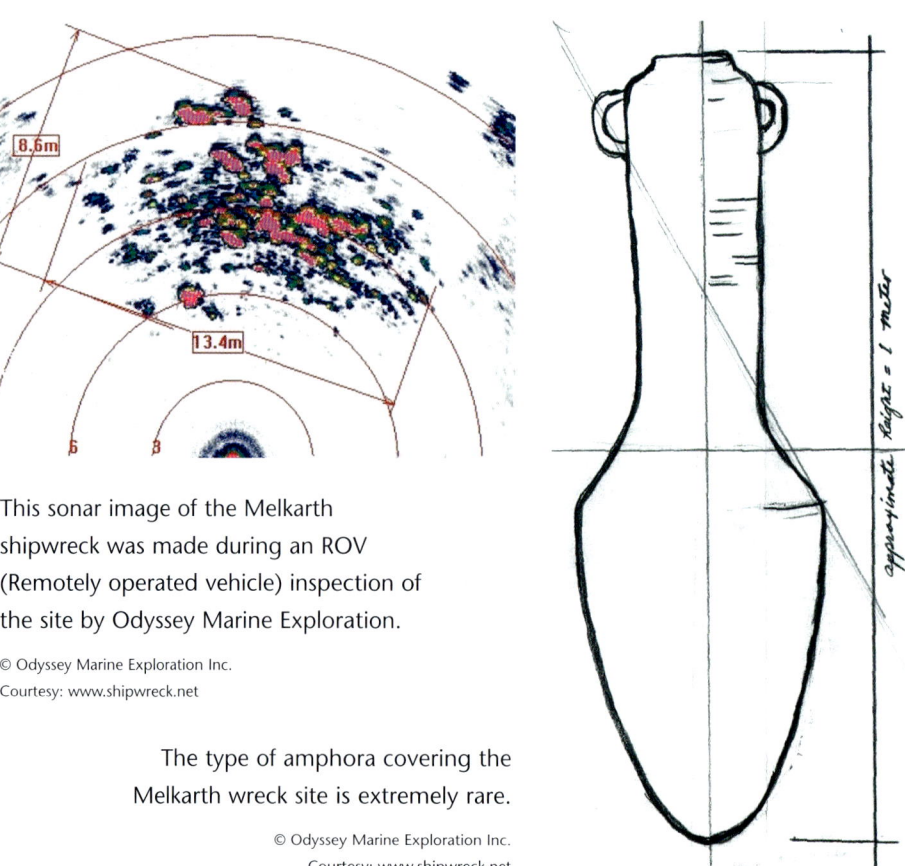

This sonar image of the Melkarth shipwreck was made during an ROV (Remotely operated vehicle) inspection of the site by Odyssey Marine Exploration.

© Odyssey Marine Exploration Inc.
Courtesy: www.shipwreck.net

The type of amphora covering the Melkarth wreck site is extremely rare.

© Odyssey Marine Exploration Inc.
Courtesy: www.shipwreck.net

I. The Phoenicians

The Melkarth shipwreck site was discovered by Odyssey Marine Exploration in 1998 almost 3000 feet below the surface of the western Mediterranean during the search for *HMS Sussex*. Melkarth is an ancient shipwreck covered by ceramic jars, or amphorae, which suggest that it was a Punic or Phoenician merchant vessel dating from between the 3rd and 5th centuries BC.

© Odyssey Marine Exploration Inc./www.shipwreck.net

The Isola Lunga (Marsala) wreck

In 1969, Sicilian dredgers discovered an ancient wreck with no apparent cargo off the island of Isola Lunga, opposite the Aegates Islands. Two years later, the British archaeologist Honor Frost, accompanied by British researchers, began investigating the site. This time, it was not a Phoenician merchant ship that the team discovered but a warship from the First Punic War, the conflict which ended in Roman victory over the Carthaginians in 241 BC.

The wood of the hull, planking and floor-timbers on excavation. They look as good as new before being darkened by oxidisation.

© Honor Frost

The wood of the hull, after treatment with polyetheleneglycol, was reassembled in a building which is now the Regional Museum at Marsala, Sicily.

© photo: Punic Ship Mission

Structure and purpose of the ship

The wreck lay buried in sand 2.5m below the surface. The dredgers first spotted a timber poking up through the sand, which Honor Frost believed to be the stern. Amazingly, it was still intact, whereas the prow and stern usually disintegrate more quickly than the hull.

The hull itself was made of pine, oak and sycamore and its planks were held together by mortise and tenon joints. An examination of the stern enabled researchers to estimate the ship's dimensions: 35 by 4.8m. This long, slender boat would have been designed for speed and been capable of carrying a large number of soldiers. Researchers concluded that it must have been a trireme, the most common type of warship in the 3rd century BC.

However, there were certain characteristics that left experts sceptical. The ship contained ballast and the keel was sheathed with lead. These two elements are commonly found in merchant vessels but very rarely in warships, since the ballast would weigh the ship down and slow its progress. These anomalies remain unexplained, as all the other clues tend to prove that this was indeed a warship built for and during the first war between the Carthaginians and the

Romans. Some bowls and plates were discovered in the wreck, for example, but no mortars, cooking pots or jars for storing water, all of which are found on merchant ships undertaking a long voyage.

Punic ship or Roman copy?

The question of its origin also remained unanswered. Was this a Carthaginian warship or a Roman copy of a Phoenician ship? As Honor Frost pointed out, the Romans had no naval tradition at this time and frequently imitated the designs of captured Carthaginian ships. Indeed, during the First Punic War, they built 100 of these replicas in less than two months.

However, certain clues encouraged researchers to favour the idea that the ship was Carthaginian. Painted inscriptions on various parts of the ship were identified as Phoenician talismanic symbols and letters of the Phoenician alphabet.

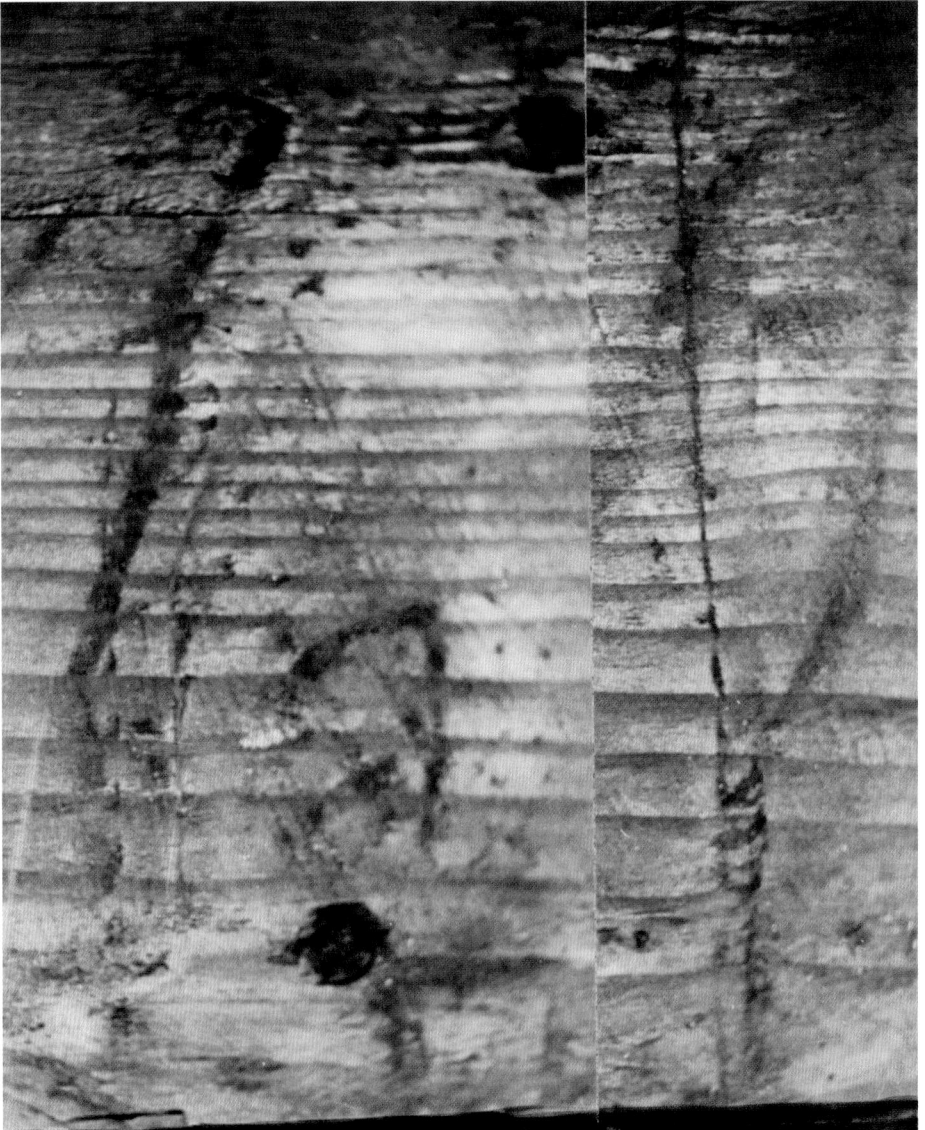

Below and right: Punic letters painted on to the hull. This is a unique discovery, because carpenter's marks are usually incised lines made by illiterate workmen, whereas the builders of this vessel seem to have been literate. Unlike hieroglyphs written on papyrus (which survive in Egypt), in the rest of the ancient world the letters that survive are on clay or stone. Phoenician calligraphy is very rare. These three letters (deduced from early semitic languages) probably form the word 'curve' (the plank on which it is written had to fit on to a curved timber).

© drawing and photo Honor Frost

Foodstuffs were found in the keel cavity and 'galley'. The photograph shows a yellow plant stem and the remains of a basket. The stem was identified as *Cannabis sativa* by the Jodrell Laboratory in London.

© Honor Frost

Constructed in haste

What did the letters mean? Quite simply, they bore witness to the ingenuity of Carthaginian carpenters, who painted symbols on each piece of the boat so that they could find them more quickly and build the vessel at record speeds – a useful device in times of war. The Isola Lunga ship would therefore have been constructed in haste to meet the demands of the conflict.

Ballast stones found with the wreck had been wrapped in fresh dunnage to protect the timbers. Some of these leaves had even retained their green colouring indicating that the ship was newly ballasted when she sank. Others were embedded in resinous material applied to the hull as waterproofing, evidence that the ship herself was new when she sank, while wood shavings conjure a picture of carpenters frantically working on the vessel up to the moment of its launch.

II. *Thalassa*, the Greek sea

Greek history is intertwined with that of the Aegean Sea and, on a larger scale, the Mediterranean. The secrets of an antiquity so closely bound up with the sea could not be unlocked by studying only ruins on land. A major slice of history lay forgotten beneath the waves until archaeologists began to explore the sea floor.

Heracles, *The Iliad*, *The Odyssey*, *The Theogony* – magical names that evoke myriad images of gods, heroes and daring sea voyages.

And yet long before Ulysses and Telemachus set sail, before the great maritime expeditions and the wave of colonisation that marked the Archaic Era,

Greek ship entering a harbour; mural from the 16th century BC.

© Gianni Dagli Orti/CORBIS

The shipwreck of Ulysses

Underwater archaeology is constantly adding to its wealth of knowledge by searching out and studying ships and cargoes fated never to reach their destinations. But what do archaeologists know about the shipwrecked sailors? Often nothing save the likelihood that they perished with their ships, victims of Aeolus and Poseidon's brutal force, especially if these deities struck far from shore, in the open sea.

Ulysses was fortunate enough to survive a storm that almost hurled him into Scylla's terrible vortex. The account of the tricks he used to cheat death make us wonder if the seafarers from our wrecks ever employed similar feats:

All of a sudden came the shrilling West, with the rushing of a great tempest, and the blast of wind snapped the two forestays of the mast, and the mast fell backward and all the gear dropped into the bilge; And behold, on the hind part of the ship the mast struck the head of the pilot and brake all the bones of his skull together, and like a diver he dropped down from the deck, and his brave spirit left his bones. In that same hour Zeus thundered and cast his bolt upon the ship, and she reeled all over being stricken by the bolt of Zeus, and was filled with sulphur, and lo, my company fell out from the vessel. Like seagulls they were borne round the black ship upon the billows, and the god reft them of returning. But I kept pacing through my ship, till the surge loosened the sides from the keel and the wave swept her along stript of her tackling, and brake her mast clean off at the keel. Now the backstay fashioned of an oxhide had been flung thereupon; therewith I lashed myself together both keel and mast, and sitting thereon I was borne by the ruinous winds.

Then verily the West Wind ceased to blow with a rushing storm, and swiftly withal the South Wind came, bringing sorrow to my soul, that so I might again measure back that space of sea, the way to deadly Charybdis. All the night was I borned but with the rising of the sun I came to the rock of Scylla, and to dread Charybdis. Now she had sucked down her salt sea water, when I was swung up on high to the tall fig-tree whereto I clung like a bat, and could find no sure rest for my feet nor place to stand, for the roots spread far below and the branches hung aloft out of reach, long and large, and overshadowed Charybdis. Steadfast I clung till she should spew forth mast and keel again; and late they came to my desire. At the hour when a man rises up from the assembly and goes to supper, one who judges the many quarrels of the young men that seek to him for law, at that same hour those timbers came forth to view from out Charybdis. And I let myself drop down hands and feet, and plunged heavily in the midst of the waters beyond the long timbers, and sitting on these I rowed hard with my hands. But the father of gods and of men suffered me no more to behold Scylla, else I should never have escaped from utter doom.

Thence for nine days was I borne, and on the tenth night the gods brought me nigh to the isle of Ogygia, where dwells Calypso of the braided tresses, an awful goddess of mortal speech, who took me in and entreated me kindly.

Bas-relief, Ulysses's ship in terracotta, from the 3rd-2nd century BC, found in Italy.

© photo: RMN, Hervé Lewandowski

equally brilliant and adventurous civilisations were making their presence felt in the Aegean. In these pre-Hellenic times, when Attica and the Peloponnese were relatively unknown, the story of the region's rise begins in Minoan Crete, so-called because of the island's legendary King Minos.

1. The odyssey of a people

Crete forms part of the mountain range extending in an arc from the Peloponnese to Anatolia. The island, one of the largest in the Mediterranean, has been inhabited since the Neolithic period. During the 3rd millennium BC, the inhabitants began working with bronze, although they lagged behind Argolis and Thessaly, and were influenced by Anatolia.

However, the growth in culture was reversed during the 24th century BC, when these advanced regions of the Aegean were invaded by less civilised peoples and plunged into barbarism.

Isolated and outlying, Crete escaped invasion, setting the stage for the island's brilliant future. Whereas the rest of the Aegean region continued to foster relations with Anatolia, Crete began looking towards the city of Byblos, itself already heavily influenced by Egypt. Although archaeologists still debate the reasons behind this sudden change, Crete blossomed towards the end of the 3rd millennium BC, and around 1900 BC became the cradle of a remarkable palace-building civilisation. Built along the northern coast (modern day Knossos and Malia) and in Messara (Phaetos), these palaces are notable as much for their originality as their complex structures, exemplified by the labyrinth in which the Minotaur was reputedly imprisoned.

The influence of Cretan civilisation spread through sea trade. Its strategic location in the eastern Mediterranean facilitated trade relations with the Peloponnese and Anatolia, and gave easy access to the Near East, Africa and Europe.

Crete exported wine, olive oil and wood, and imported wheat, but it traded primarily in luxury goods. The Minoans took painted pottery, brightly coloured cloth, jewellery and bronze weapons to Melos, Mycenae, Cyprus and Egypt. Their ships returned from Egypt laden with semi-precious stones and, in particular, amethysts used for making seals. In Cyprus, they loaded copper ingots, and in Melos and Yali filled their holds with obsidian.

The whole Aegean region began to imitate Cretan art and its multicoloured Camares pottery, jewellery and seals engraved on precious stones. By the 15th century BC, Minoan-inspired culture had spread across the entire southern part of the Aegean world, to the extent that archaeologists often find it difficult to establish whether a particular vase found in Mycenae, Pylos or on the island of Melos was imported from Crete or made locally.

However, around 1700 BC, a cataclysmic event sealed the fate of Minoan thalassocracy (or sovereignty of the seas). The island of Thera (modern day Santorini) was rocked by violent volcanic eruptions causing a tidal wave and

Cretan statuette. The nudity and proportions of this female figure indicate the emergence of the Geometric period. In bronze, dating from the beginning of the Recent Minoan III period (1400-1050 BC).

© photo: RMN, Hervé Lewandowski

Master seafarers

A large Minoan jar (Middle Minoan) decorated with scroll and floral motifs in the archaeological museum in Heracleion, Greece.

© Roger Wood/CORBIS

Creto-Mycenaean terracotta *rhyton* (drinking cup) in the shape of a hedgehog, from the 2nd millennium BC. Found in Syria, at Minet el Beida.

© photo: RMN, Hervé Lewandowski

earthquakes that struck Crete, devastating the east and centre of the island. The Minoans never recovered from the disaster and shortly afterwards, the Achaeans (or Mycenaeans), who had already settled in Argolis, took advantage of the former's weakened state to encircle Crete and peacefully, but definitively supplant the first great Aegean civilisation.

The golden age of Mycenae

Although Mycenaean domination of the Aegean was not achieved until around 1400 BC, its expansion had already begun two centuries earlier. The Mycenaeans, who took their name from their most famous city, were well accustomed to trading alongside the Minoans as early as the 16th century BC. Mycenaean navigators took over moorings from their Minoan neighbours. Consequently, it is not uncommon to find fragments of Mycenaean and Minoan pottery from the same period on the Aeolian Islands or at Rhodes. The Achaeans followed in the footsteps of the Cretans, going as far as Egypt and Syria in their turn. After the fall of Minoan Crete, the Mycenaean fleet quite simply stepped into the breach left by its Cretan counterpart in eastern Mediterranean trading relations.

This civilisation reached its zenith in the 13th century BC, as reported by Hittite sources, who compared its power with that of Egypt. However, a darker period began for the Mycenaeans around 1230 BC. The Dorians, an Indo-European race from the north, arrived and laid waste to the continent's main Mycenaean cities, setting fire to Mycenae, Pylos and Tiryns. They gradually subjugated the islands of the Aegean Sea, Crete and the Mediterranean region. In Anatolia, the Hittite Empire collapsed, and further south, Enkomi in Cyprus and Ugarit on the Syrian coast were razed. The Achaeans took refuge in the mountains of the northern islands of the Peloponnese or fled towards Rhodes and Cyprus.

Thus began the darkest period in the history of Greece. Its links with the Near East were severed. All that remained was a disparate group of small, weakened, inward-looking states, a configuration that the next era would see develop into a new type of nation: the city-state. Another 400 years would pass before Greece rose from its ashes and once more looked to the sea.

Greek expansion from the Archaic Era onwards

Greek influence began to spread in the middle of the 8th century BC. Some historians, however, see the era as a period of precolonisation for the Aegean area. It is true that the Dorians' arrival led indirectly to the establishment of other Greek settlements on the coasts of Asia Minor; nevertheless, it remains difficult to regard them as genuine colonies.

During the 8th century BC, Greece enjoyed a political and cultural renaissance which saw the beginnings of colonisation in the Mediterranean basin and economic expansion, which would last for three centuries. There were two reasons people chose to emigrate – trade and land – and three areas they emigrated from: regions with poor soil such as Achaea or Dorida, trading regions such as the Corinthian peninsula and the cities of Asia Minor, and those experiencing internal unrest.

The lust for land can be easily explained by the fact that both mainland Greece and its islands suffered from overpopulation and its infertile territories, plagued by periods of drought, could no longer provide sufficient food for its people. In addition, political unrest often drove the weakest clans into exile to escape stronger rivals.

Trade also provided a strong incentive for the Greeks to occupy other regions in their search for raw materials such as grain, metals and wood for construction. Like the Phoenicians, they chose to settle around well-sheltered, easily defensible harbours.

Greek colonists were scattered virtually everywhere:
- To the east: The Greeks settled in the north of Syria, Phoenicia and Cyprus. Al Mina, a large trading centre at the mouth of the Orontes river, first used by the Euboeans and later by the Milesians, became the leading city in the region, thus guaranteeing the Greeks an opening into Syria, Assyria and the other Mesopotamian kingdoms.
- To the west: Greek interest in the west dates back to the Mycenaean era, when some navigators reached the shores of Italy but did not settle there.

II. Thalassa, the Greek sea

Naxos in Sicily was founded in 734 BC, followed by Catana, Zankle (modern day Messina), Syracuse, Gela, Selinus and Akragas (Agrigento). The Greeks settled on the west coast of Italy at Cumea, Pithekoussai (Ischia), Poseidonia and Elea. These regions were accessed by coastal vessels which crossed the Otranto channel and followed the southern coast of Italy. It was also possible to make a direct crossing of the Ionian Sea from the Peloponnese.

The natural resources of the colonies in the southern part of the Italian peninsula led to them becoming known as Greater Greece. The region became a hub for trade, on which it prospered. The Greeks exchanged the wheat they imported from these western regions for all kinds of pottery, such as *kraters*, *hydriae*, amphorae, goblets and even ordinary tableware.

Further west, the Phocaeans began the colonisation of the coastal area in 600 BC with the founding of Massilia (modern day Marseilles). To make their voyages more cost-efficient, hardy Phocaean seafarers were happy to sail in penteconters, long boats with 50 oars that other Greek peoples tended to use only as warships.

The French ministry of culture's department for underwater archaeological research, or DRASSM (Département des recherches archéologiques subaquatiques et sous-marines), discovered the wreck of such a boat off the island of Porquerolles, in southern France, which they named Pointe Lequin 1A, dating from the second half of the 6th century BC. Archaeologists found a batch of wine amphorae, tableware and drinking goblets with black Ionian and Attic figures stacked in earthenware jars. Among these was an Ionian goblet, which

Fragment of a Greek pot found on the site of the Pointe Lequin 1A wreck. The figures probably represent Theseus and the Minotaur.

© DRASSM

Master seafarers

Legend

- ■ Greek colonies
- □ Greek cities
- ● Carthaginian cities
- ▨ the Persian Empire around 480 BC
- ▨ areas where Greek goods were traded
- ▨ Greek settlement
- ● major trading centres
- ～ limit of Carthaginian influence mid 5th century BC
- ⌒ trading routes

Greek expansion from the 8th to 6th centuries BC

© Periplus Publishing London Ltd. Graphics : Yann Bernard

II. Thalassa, *the Greek sea*

depicted Theseus and the Minotaur. The cargo also included lamps, Attic amphorae, vases and statuettes most of which originated in eastern Greece.

In the north, the Greeks established colonies along the eastern shores of the Adriatic (most notably on Corfu), on the northern coast of the Aegean Sea and the Euxine Sea (now the Black Sea). It was the Milesians in particular who settled along the shores of the Euxine, where they were able to acquire supplies of wood, metals and amber.

The southern Mediterranean coast

In the southern Mediterranean, the Greeks travelled to Cyrene and Egypt, taking either the direct route from Crete, Carpathos or Rhodes, or going via Cyprus and along the coast.

Cyrene was founded by the inhabitants of Thera during the second half of the 7th century BC. Egypt, with whom the Greeks carried out considerable trade, granted them some land on the Pelusian branch of the Nile and opened the gates of the city of Naucratis to them. Because those who settled there came primarily from Miletus, Chios, Rhodes and even Phocaea, it is hardly surprising that Egyptian waters abound in Greek remains.

On the site of the ancient city of Heracleion off Aboukir in Egypt, Franck Goddio and his team recently located the wrecks of at least 10 Greek ships dating from the 6th century BC. They found a small object, probably the pedestal for a statue, with a Greek epitaph. They also discovered a stele which was identical in every way to the one from Naucratis, discovered in 1899 and dating from 380 BC. It bore an engraving in hieroglyphics of a decree by Nectanebo I, founder of the 30th Dynasty, who levied a tax on the activities of the Greeks trading in Naucratis and gave the revenue to the treasury of the temple to the goddess Neith. The text of the inscription is as follows:

"Then His Majesty said: 'Let one tenth of the gold, silver, wood and joinery and all things coming from the Greek Sea, be taxed for the King's House in the place called Hone, as well as one tenth of the gold, silver and all things existing in the domain of the harbour named Kratj on the bank of the Anu canal.' "

Athens: the birth of an empire

Although Athens was one of the richest and most powerful cities in Greece at the dawn of the 5th century BC, its maritime activities contributed nothing to its influence and it had played no part in the colonisation that characterised the Archaic Era. Judging by the harbour it established at Phaleron, east of Piraeus, which was impossible to defend, Athens showed little more than a passing interest in the sea.

The threat from Persia during the early part of the 5th century BC prompted the ambitious general and statesman Themistocles to equip the city with a sizeable fleet of warships whose role was crucial in the battles against Sparta.

Having emerged triumphant from the Median Wars, Athens craved yet more power. It took advantage of its enemies' disarray to colonise strategic regions and liberate Greek populations in Asia. Strengthened by its newfound status as seapower and defender of Greek colonies, it founded the Delean League in 478 BC as a defensive alliance against the Persians. The first to sign the treaty were Samos, Chios, Lesbos, Delos and some cities from the Cyclades who, in exchange for protection, were obliged to provide the Athenian fleet with ships and money.

Shortly afterwards, Cimon embarked on an aggressive and imperialistic foreign policy. He fought to strengthen the league's position in the Aegean Sea, winning numerous victories, and also advocated taking military action against rebellious cities (Naxos in 470 BC and Thassos in 465 BC). The transfer of the league's treasury from Delos to Athens in 454 BC marked the transition from confederacy to empire. The successors to Cimon, Ephialtes and Pericles, supported this policy of territorial annexation, particularly in the Euxine Sea region for its wheat, in Egypt and in southern Italy. Athens reached its zenith and acquired superiority in all domains. The Thirty-Year Peace with the Persians brought about the end of its land-based empire, but left Athens with its maritime supremacy unchallenged.

Sparta grew concerned at this expansion, leading to the Peloponnesian War when Athens attempted to gain control of part of central Greece. Twenty-five years later, weakened by conflict, siege and starvation, Athens agreed to the terms for peace: the destruction of the Long Walls and those of Piraeus. Its fleet surrendered in 404 BC, leaving Sparta to become an influential force in the ancient world.

A power struggle then began between Sparta and Thebes, but this bloody contest for supremacy left both protagonists dispirited. Athens, for its part, formed a Second Delean League in 377 BC, once more giving it control of the sea for a short period of time. The ascension of Philip II to the throne of Macedonia in 359 BC marked the decline of the imperialist city-state. Revolts against the second confederacy (Chios, Kos and Rhodes in 357 BC) succeeded in breaking the treaties, and resulted in Philip gaining control of the whole of Greece. The city of Athens retained its autonomy but had to sign the Corinthian League treaty, which grouped together all Greek cities under the hegemony of Macedonia. The glory of Athens was at an end, leaving Philip to pave the way for the conquests of his son, Alexander the Great.

Centuries of war and instability drove many cities to take to the seas. Athenian imperialism, as has been demonstrated, was characterised by the development of its maritime activity. Harbours were constructed, ships were built and perfected, including the famous triremes, and not surprisingly in these troubled times of war and natural disasters, many sank.

In the early 20th century, archaeologists and historians began rediscovering long-forgotten relics from a bloody but fascinating age. Reminders of Athenian imperialism, as well as that of Philip and Alexander the Great, can be found throughout the Mediterranean, as far as Egypt, where ongoing excavations regularly uncover remarkable finds.

Bust of the Athenian statesman Pericles, who lived during the 5th century BC, the 'Century of Pericles'.

© Bettmann / CORBIS

Master seafarers

Map of the Aegean Sea, with Greek cities in italics.

© Periplus Publishing London Ltd. Graphics: Yann Bernard

Poseidon, god of the sea

Hesiod's *The Theogony* tells how Poseidon, Zeus and Hades, having usurped their father Cronos, drew straws to share out the dominions of the world. Zeus won the sky, Hades the shadows of the underworld and Poseidon the sea, the land having been deemed common territory. Poseidon was jealous of his brothers' power, and became quarrelsome and cruel, and these traits were reflected in the savagery of the elements at sea. Although theoretically god of all the sea, he is more associated with tempests than calm seas and the ancients invoked him mainly when in danger.

Underwater archaeology in Greece

The first underwater archaeological mission began in 1884 under the direction of Christos Tsountas in the strait situated between Salamis and Attica, where the Athenian fleet defeated the Persians in 480 BC. The excavation was supervised by the Athens Archaeological Society but methods at that time were not developed enough to yield much in the way of results. Sponge fishermen played a vital role in the discovery of remains and were responsible for triggering most of the excavations that took place by bringing their finds to the attention of the state or archaeologists.

In the early 20th century, some scientists began to take an interest in how the coast had changed over time, which enabled them to envisage new possibilities for the discipline of archaeology. They identified submerged harbours which were invisible to the naked eye as they were buried under layers of sediment.

The rapid development of diving technologies opened new doors for underwater archaeology and made it possible for archaeologists to work at hitherto unexplored depths. Interest in underwater archaeology has greatly increased in Greece since the end of the Second World War and several institutions were founded during the 1970s, including HIMA (the Hellenic Institute of Marine Archaeology) in 1973 and the Ephorate of Underwater Antiquities in 1976.

The number of finds has increased as a result and many wrecks have been excavated and studied, providing invaluable historical information. Archaeology is therefore helping us to discover an entire portion of Greek history. Naval architecture, military ports and shipwreck cargoes combined with the study of ancient texts and land-based sites, provide an invaluable insight into the trade and colonisation that characterised this period in Greek history.

2. Harbour sites

The sites of ports were chosen for strategic reasons. Natural areas of shelter were fashioned into basins, quays, jetties and boat sheds, some with the addition of defensive walls. Most of these constructions are now submerged, but underwater archaeology allows us to rediscover and study their ingenious and varied architecture.

The sanctuary of Halieis

Halieis was a small Peloponnesian port situated on the southernmost tip of the Argolic peninsula, protected by fortified walls and a citadel. During the Archaic Era (7th-6th century BC), this city-state was important enough to mint its own coins.

Halieis suffered the consequences of the long years of war between Athens and Sparta. Weakened by the outbreak of the Peloponnesian war in 431 BC, it was forced to sign a treaty in 424 BC giving Athens the right to use its harbour for the duration of the war. The city was abandoned after the death of Alexander the Great in 323 BC. The walls surrounding the citadel were destroyed a few decades later and several centuries would pass before it was occupied by the Romans.

Luckily the ruins of this historic city, opposite the entrance to the bay, remained undisturbed by the construction of the modern town of Porto Cheli. Halieis is therefore rich in material for archaeologists.

An American team commenced excavations in 1962 and divided the site into four levels. At the top of the hill was the citadel. Below that was a site containing several workshops, most probably for the manufacture of dyes. On the lowest level were workshops for minting coins as well as the ruins of houses and streets. The surprising number of land-based and underwater ruins transformed this archaeological mission into an enormous project lasting almost 20 years.

The ruins at Halieis are clearly visible owing to the harbour's shallow depth.

© Amy C. Smith

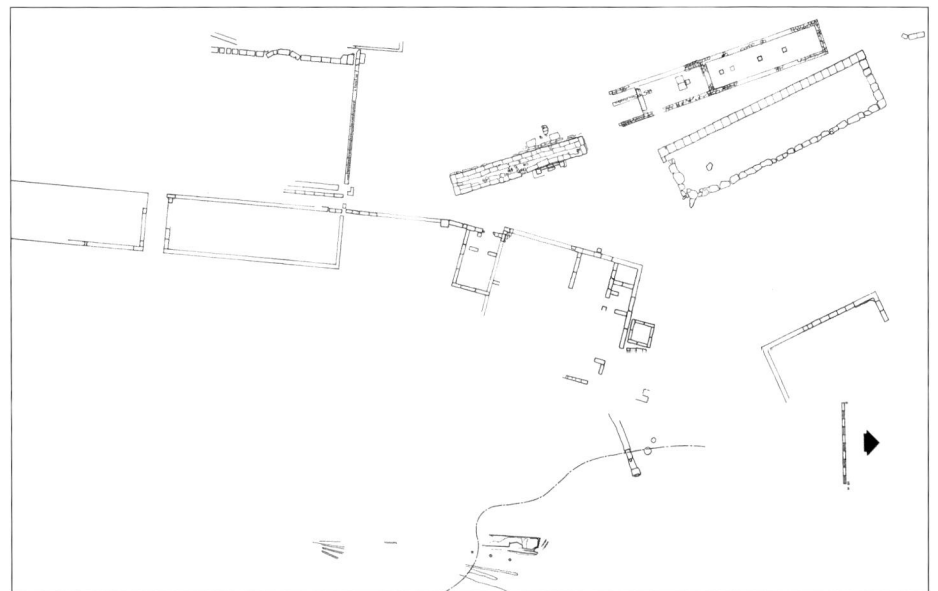
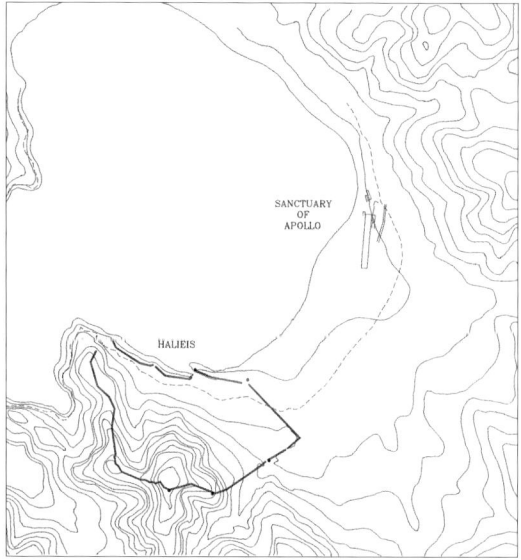

Plans of the sanctuary of Halieis.
© Halieis Excavations Publication Committee

Excavation of the underwater ruins

A preliminary survey enabled the team to draw up an excavation plan and a map of the site. When the weather was fine, the ruins could be easily seen in the clear water, revealing the foundations of a sanctuary with an altar for animal sacrifices, two temples, one more recent than the other, and several additional buildings, as well as a stadium.

Some clues suggest that the sanctuary was dedicated to Apollo, the god of beauty and the arts. In Greek mythology, Apollo was a deity descended from the Titans, the son of Zeus and Leto, and a member of the second generation of Olympic gods. The twin brother of Artemis, he was the most handsome of the twelve greater gods of Olympus. Ancient literary sources referred to Apollo as the god of Halieis, an assumption confirmed by the presence of local coins bearing his effigy. In addition, the text of a treaty between Athens and Halieis, engraved in stone and dated to 423 BC, contains instructions to take a copy of this same treaty to Apollo's sanctuary in Halieis. Any doubt about the divinity's identity was completely dispelled by the discovery of three lightly corroded iron rods that were identified as the three keys to the temple. One of them was inscribed with the name Apollo but only the letter 'A' was still visible. Greek works of art often portray priests carrying keys of this type.

After three seasons of excavations, the team was finally able to piece together the history of the sanctuary at Halieis. The temple of Apollo, a long, narrow structure, had been built around 780 BC at right angles to a straight, level track intended for athletic games. It was 27m long and 4.5m wide. The temple was separated from the track by an altar. Other buildings were added later, including one to the east of the altar made up of several small rooms that would have been used for dining during religious festivals or during the games. This was suggested by the many fragments of goblets found by the well adjacent to the building. Other constructions from the same period, including the second temple close to the site of the original one, had been built on higher ground and

Coin bearing the head of Apollo.

© Araldo de Luca/CORBIS

therefore failed to survive the ravages of time because they were not submerged.

The first temple was by far the best preserved monument on the site. It was built of roughly hewn limestone blocks and its roof clad with baked clay tiles. The inside, which had a central row of wooden columns, comprised three rooms. The room nearest the entrance housed a panel, now faded, depicting Apollo. A marble statue was also discovered in this room but because it was completed much later than the temple, it is thought to be a copy of the original statue. The temple treasury, located between the pedestal and the back wall, yielded finds including 18 silver coins minted between 550 and 525 BC, fragments of amber imported from the Baltic, ostrich eggshells from Africa and an engraved bronze plaque from the early 5th century BC with a partially obliterated inscription. The lines of the text that are still visible mention a fine, which is no doubt a warning not to misappropriate the treasure kept in the temple. Many of the coins discovered were imprinted with a palm tree, the symbol of Tiryns, whose inhabitants arrived in Halieis during the previous century.

The presence of animal horns and bones indicated that the middle room was reserved for purification rituals. Three bronze animal figurines were also found, as well as an altar erected in honour of Apollo, made of horns piled on top of one another.

The end room, where the offerings were kept, revealed fragments of over 5,000 miniature goblets, knives, spears and swords.

The temple underwent some renovation in the 5th century BC. A side entrance was added, with an elegant stone landing leading to it, and the old circular columns were replaced by wooden pillars. Additional columns, erected without following any specific plan, were undoubtedly intended to support the roof, which was in danger of collapsing. The temple was abandoned at the end of the 5th century BC before finally being destroyed by fire a short time later.

Meanwhile, Halieis, which had become a prosperous, flourishing city, decided to use part of its wealth to benefit the sanctuary. The altar facing the former temple was rebuilt and enlarged, and a canopy supported by four columns was erected at one end. Another monument was also built nearby. The discovery of goblets and iron weapons indicated that this was a temple, which had almost certainly been built to replace the original temple of Apollo.

The stadium consisted of a running track measuring only 167m in length – one of the shortest ever found in Greece, with the starting and finishing lines still visible. Finally, a small Roman thermal spa was discovered, confirming a period, albeit brief, of Roman occupation.

There is nothing to suggest why the sanctuary and the town of Halieis were abandoned around 323 BC. A rise in sea level could not have been the cause because the sanctuary was not claimed by the sea for another 400 years. A more plausible hypothesis is that a rival power viewed the naval base at Halieis as a threat and decided to destroy it, forcing the inhabitants to flee the city.

The Halieis excavation

Karl M. Petruso

Halieis is located at the southwestern tip of the Argolid peninsula in southern Greece, near the modern town of Porto Cheli. The site shows evidence of sporadic occupation in the Neolithic and Bronze Ages as well as the Early Iron Age (5th-early 1st millennium BC). A small city (with a population estimated at a few thousand) flourished here in the 5th and 4th centuries BC on gently sloping terraces rising above the southern shore of a large oval bay (currently about 1.5km by 1km). There was a strategic advantage to be had by founding a city here: the hills south of the bay (where the city's acropolis was sited) provide a commanding view of the strait and the island of Spetses to the south. The settlement of Halieis was excavated by an American team from the late 1950s to the late 1970s. Its domestic architecture has provided an illuminating glimpse into everyday life in a typical rural settlement of the classical period.

Halieis was settled in the early 5th century BC by refugees from Tiryns, a city at the northern end of the Argolic Gulf. While Halieis received occasional mention in the accounts of the classical historians Herodotus, Thucydides and Xenophon, it was never a player in significant events of the Peloponnesian Wars. The city was attacked unsuccessfully by Athens in 460 BC, and was captured by Sparta in about 430 BC. A few years later, during the first Peloponnesian War, Halieis struck a treaty with Athens, whose navy defended its harbour to the end of the war. In the following century, Halieis allied itself with Sparta.

As a result largely of geological subsidence over the past 2,000 years, the buildings constructed in Antiquity at the edge of the sea are now submerged under some 2m of water. Following preliminary investigations using a fishing boat and snorkel gear, excavations took place in the late 1960s and early 1970s under the direction of Michael H. Jameson, then of the University of Pennsylvania. The present author was one of more than a dozen university students who, together with professional archaeologists and technical specialists, took part in the explorations of the underwater remains of the site at that time.

Water conditions presented a challenge. The stillness of this enclosed body of water necessitated slow and careful swimming while carrying out reconnaissance and excavation, since even the slightest motion stirred up clouds of fine silt which might obscure visibility for an hour or more. After experimenting with several mechanical devices to clear the silt from the architecture, it was finally determined that a dredge powered by generators (run from a fishing boat) was ideal. The dredge acted like a vacuum cleaner – the diver would aim its mouth at silt, vegetation and small rocks, which were sucked in and discharged via a long pipe into the middle of the bay.

Two areas on the southern and eastern edges of the bay attracted the

Aerial view of the sanctuary of Apollo at Halieis. In the lower left-hand corner can be seen the starting line for the racecourse and the spectators' arena. In the north, the two almost parallel temples dating from the 7th and 6th centuries BC. The sacrificial altar is to the south of these. The photograph, by Julian and Eunice Whittlesey, was taken with a camera suspended from a balloon.

© Halieis Excavations Publication Committee

expedition's interest. First was the harbour complex. The installations here included a 90m stretch of the city wall and two opposing massive round towers (each 9.2m in diameter and about 20m apart). Clues to the existence of these facilities were obtained from aerial photography and confirmed by sonar profiling. Snorkelers then used poles to probe beneath the silt to check the locations, depths and directions of the walls for plotting on the site plan. The archaeologist interpreted the two round towers as the entrance to a small enclosed military harbour and quay. Pottery found in the packing for the wall near the south tower suggests a 5th century BC date for construction of this part of the harbour complex.

The second area of interest, on the east side of the bay, consisted of a number of large structures that were not at first identifiable. As the silt was dredged away, a limestone platform emerged near a pair of long and narrow buildings. The platform was eventually recognised as the foundations of an altar, and – as is the case with early classical Greek religious complexes –

Three keys to the temple of Apollo, fused over time into a single block. One is inscribed with the name of Apollo. The letter 'A' is visible, the remaining letters less so.

© James Dengate

the buildings before which it stands were identified as temples.

The earlier of the two was a very narrow tripartite structure containing a single line of interior column bases. Its proportions, as well as pottery fragments and a radiocarbon date from a pine timber excavated *in situ*, suggest a date in the late 8th century or early 7th century BC, which would make it one of the oldest stone temples in the Greek world. The identity of the deity to whom the sanctuary was dedicated is suggested by an inscription dated to 423 BC, decreeing that a treaty between Halieis and Athens be erected in the sanctuary of the god Apollo at Halieis. This inscription, together with excavated fragments of a marble cult statue of a nude male as well as a corroded iron key bearing the name Apollo, strongly suggest that this complex was in fact the city's sanctuary to Apollo.

A noteworthy discovery among the outbuildings of the sanctuary just to the south of the altar was a line of blocks, each of which bears two parallel grooves and a square posthole. Such rows of blocks are known from many other Greek cities (including Nemea and Isthmia not far to the north, where they are very well preserved): they are the starting lines of ancient stadiums. By probing in the silt along a line perpendicular to the starting line, divers followed a row of limestone foundation blocks marking the eastern side of the stadium some 167m to the south, where the opposite starting line was excavated.

The harbour at Halieis is among the finest natural ports in the entire Mediterranean. It is not at all surprising, then, that both the Athenians and the Spartans should have sought to command it. The mouth to the bay was less than 250m wide in Antiquity, making it easily defensible. The channel was deep enough to accommodate the keels and holds of large-draft vessels. Ships rounding the Peloponnese en route to or from Piraeus (the port of Athens) could take shelter within the harbour when squalls arose without notice, as frequently occurs during the sailing season; surely this feature made Halieis as attractive to sailors in Antiquity as it is today. Ironically, the very submerging of the coastal sectors of the ancient city ensured their survival for scientific investigation, inasmuch as Porto Cheli – now dominated by many hotels and a yacht marina on the northwest side of the bay – has been intensively developed for tourism.

The submerged harbour of Samos

The island of Samos enjoys an advantageous position in the eastern Aegean Sea. The town of Samos was built in the Pythagorean region and has no connection with the modern town of the same name. From earliest times through to the Middle Ages, the island played a major role in the political and economic life of Greece. In 535 BC, the tyrant Polycratus seized power and immediately ordered a naval fleet of 100 vessels to be built, using it to establish Samos's supremacy in the Aegean Sea. It was during this period that the city's fortifications were built along with the two harbour installations to the east and west of the town.

The Samians, who were renowned metalworkers and silversmiths, exported their wares throughout the Mediterranean as far as Spain. Between 479 and 366 BC, the island was conquered first by the Persians and then by the Athenians. It came under Roman rule in 129 BC, and later became part of the Byzantine Empire. It was repeatedly pillaged and destroyed by pirates.

The underwater excavations of Samos began in 1988 with a team of archaeological divers led by Angeliki Simossi, and continued in 1993 and 1994.

The harbour of Samos was located in a sheltered bay at the foot of Mount Ambelos. It was east of the ancient city and was a closed harbour, formed by the continuation of the city walls into the sea.

Archaeologists were particularly interested in the southern part of the harbour basin, which the local authorities planned to develop. They consulted a number of ancient texts as a starting point for their excavation, relying on passages from Herodotus, Pliny, Thucydides and Strabo.

When the site was excavated, it became clear that many parts of the modern harbour had been built on ancient foundations. This was the case with the north wall, the south jetty and the southern sea wall. The latter had been built on top of a 480m-long stone structure which was an ancient breakwater lying about 3m from the shore.

Another stone structure was discovered to the north of the modern harbour at a depth of 2m; it was between 170m and 190m long and 20m wide. This structure may have been part of a sea wall that extended the land-based fortifications from north to south. The sea wall would have protected ships at anchor in the harbour from the swell and the southerly winds. The breakwater would also have served as a defensive wall. No trace remains of ship sheds, although their presence is mentioned in several ancient texts.

The breakwater seems to date from the ancient Hellenistic period, around the end of the 4th century BC. This appeared to be confirmed by pottery discovered in a layer of organic material which had formed on top of the foundation wall, as all the fragments were from the Hellenistic period or later. However, more recent research suggests that the harbour was constructed by Polycrates in the 6th century BC and was one of the most important in Ancient Greece.

Archaeologists discovered a quay dating from the Archaic Era abutting onto the breakwater. Proof of its age came with the discovery of two bowls (or

Aerial view of the ancient city of Samos in Greece.

© Yann Arthus-Bertrand / CORBIS

lekanides) from the 5th and 6th centuries BC, just prior to the Hellenistic phase of construction.

Excavating a harbour often leads to the discovery of a variety of objects thrown from ships or quays. Their location in the harbour makes them invaluable tools for dating harbour installations. Archaeologists discovered pottery from a wide range of places and periods, ranging from the Archaic to the Hellenistic eras. This included an intact 54cm tall Late Roman I amphora with a shoulder and base encircled by a series of grooves similar to the teeth of a comb, which confirmed a Roman presence. Other similar fragments of amphorae were found dating from the 4th to the 6th century AD.

Finds also included an almost complete Africana II A amphora from the 3rd century BC, cups without handles from the same period, assorted tableware from the 2nd century BC, fragments of Rhodian amphorae from the 2nd century BC and most exciting of all, a beautiful terracotta statuette of a bull with raised head dating from the 1st century BC.

All these finds help us to appreciate the importance of the harbour on Samos in ancient times. The discoveries provide proof that Samos was occupied by various regimes down through the ages. As for the harbour itself, we must await a complete topographical survey to say with accuracy when it was constructed.

The antique ports of Thassos

Angeliki Simossi

During Antiquity, the city of Thassos had two harbours, the merchant harbour in the north and the military harbour in the south. The merchant harbour possessed a mole which stretched more than 110m to the west. This 18m wide construction had a bulge at the end where a semicircular tower, 20m in diameter, once stood.

This impressive construction appears to be contemporary with the city's outer wall, from around 500 BC, and was maintained in good repair until the city's destruction in the 7th century AD. Protected by this man-made breakwater, the merchant harbour received ships at the base of the city walls, where two gates led into the sanctuary of Poseidon, the protector of seafarers.

The ancient closed, military harbour which accommodated the long vessels destined for combat or more protracted voyages, was identified in the 19th century. At the time of its construction, this harbour was identical to the first, but with a predetermined military purpose. Because of this, and its proximity to the city walls, it was fortified with a narrow, well protected access. Underwater excavation was difficult between D and F (see map) and was limited to a few soundings towards the interior of the harbour basin, which was identified as early Christian. Only one older construction, composed of horizontally joined marble blocks, was found below this level, at point E.

The entrance at that time was not as we see it today and access was via the northern corner. In this first version of the harbour, only segment CD was open, reached through a narrow passage that allowed triremes to slip through and could be closed by a chain. An unbroken wall in DEFG fortified the side facing the sea. Corner access was common in ancient naval harbours: at Samos; the Archaic harbour of the tyrant Polycrates; and later at Phalasarna in Crete and Amathus in Cyprus. In the case of Thassos, the opening at CD had the advantage of being protected by the mole to the north of the merchant harbour. The wall surrounding this harbour, a high rampart joined to the city wall, dated from the 5th century BC. At ABC and FGH, it can be directly observed that the two arms which formed it were built using large marble blocks with bosses identical to those used in the city wall, erected around 500 BC, as demonstrated by numerous excavations and probes. The powerful link, still perfectly visible at A, between the harbour wall and the city wall, was proof of a unique method of construction.

Ship sheds (*neosoikoi*) were an essential part of ancient naval harbours. Traces of these sheds, long enough to house 36m triremes, were found in the corner ABC near BC. The foundations, dating from the first half of the 5th century BC (two successive phases were identified), belonged to edifices which would have created a series of saw tooth roofs, with three boats to each shed. The ancient historians Herodotus and Thucydides testified to the existence of Thassos's fleet of warships at the beginning of the 5th century BC.

II. Thalassa, the Greek sea

According to Pliny, the inhabitants of Thassos were the first to use triremes. It suffered the loss of 33 warships in 465 BC – but was still powerful enough to withstand a lengthy siege, leading to the conclusion that the number of ships accommodated by the closed harbour must have been greater than this and probably as many as 45 or 50. This means that there must have been at least 15 ship sheds, each housing three triremes, in the closed harbour at Thassos.

These ship sheds were comparable with the *neosoikoi* discovered during excavations in other Greek cities, but these are from a later date. Thassos, along with Piraeus, is therefore one of the earliest examples found. At the end of the 4th century BC, the closed harbour's fortifications were strengthened at its vulnerable points by the addition of round towers. At B and C, the foundations of two of these towers can be seen in shallow water and their presence, particularly in the case of tower C, can only be explained if the harbour entrance was in this sector. The base of another round tower was found at G in a better state of preservation.

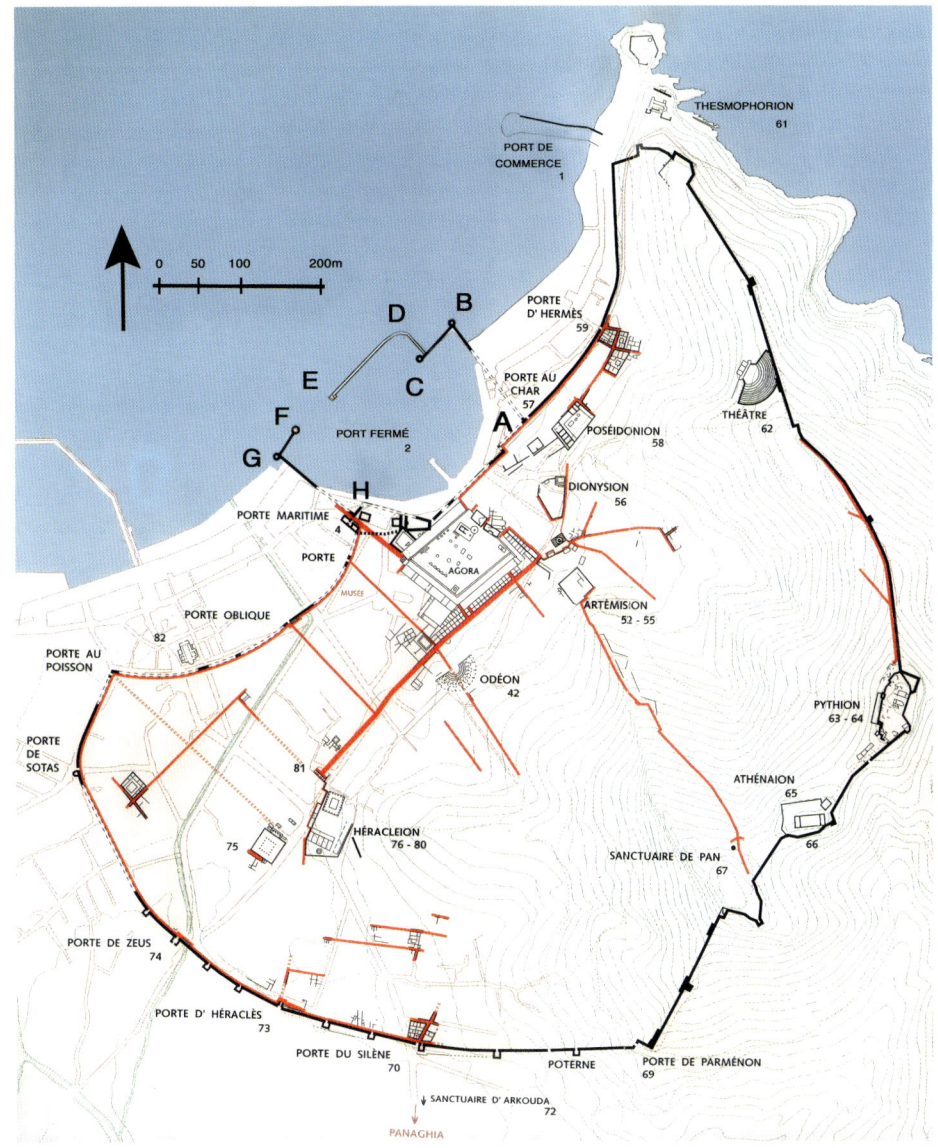

Map showing the outline of ancient Thassos.

© EFA, T. Kozelj and Wurch-Kozelj

Underwater excavation of the harbour at Thassos

The island of Thassos was situated in the northern Aegean Sea not far from the coast of Thrace. Colonised by Ionian emigrants from Paros during the 8th century BC, the city of Thassos grew rapidly and became extremely prosperous in the 6th century BC. It was protected by a marble wall, connected to a fortified bridge with a second, open harbour stretching to the north.

Following the Median Wars, Athens forced Thassos to join the Athenian Confederacy or Delean League. This defensive alliance, set up by Athens in 478 BC, grouped together Aegean cities who, in principle, retained their independence from Athens. Despite numerous wars, the merchants of Thassos continued to prosper, which helped to foster trade between Thrace and the Greek world during the 2nd and 1st centuries BC.

The harbour at Thassos is very well preserved and so is extremely interesting to archaeologists. The first excavation was carried out by the Greek Ephorate of Underwater Antiquities between 1980 and 1984. An archaeological mission on a much larger scale, aimed at surveying the military and merchant harbours, was then launched in cooperation with the École Française in Athens.

Numerous literary documents (Herodotus, Xenophon, Plutarch and Pliny)

A stele from the port.

© EFA, Philippe Collet

Relief from the gate, depicting the goddess driving a chariot.

© EFA, T. Kozelj

indicated that the city had both an open and a closed harbour. The latter, which was separated from the town by a surrounding wall, was designed for military purposes and only accommodated warships.

Although exploration was particularly difficult owing to the harbour's murky water, the divers' efforts were rewarded by some wonderful and unexpected finds.

The ruins of the closed harbour are situated in the eastern part of the old town. Exploration of the site revealed that the layout of the modern quays partially followed that of the ancient harbour wall. In places, the quays had actually been built on top of the original wall foundations. Two towers had been erected on either side of the channel, with another two that stood at the ends of the two moles surrounding the harbour entrance. The entrance itself was 20m wide and positioned on a corner. The basin in the military harbour was quadrilateral in shape with an actual depth of 3m. The merchant harbour, which opened to the south, witnessed considerable trading.

Beyond the western walls, archaeologists located an extension made from large slabs of schist alternating with marble blocks fixed together using double dovetail mortises. This formed a kind of artificial beach dating from the Hellenistic age. They also found a sanctuary in this part of the harbour which may have been dedicated to Artemis. The harbour, as it is today, was built during the early Christian era with the dimensions unchanged.

The excavation also provided the opportunity to raise a variety of artefacts,

Underwater view of the breakwater protecting the northern harbour.

© EFA, Jean-Yves Empereur

Boat sheds in the submerged inner port at Thassos.

© EFA, Jean-Yves Empereur

from the Archaic Era through to the Byzantine period. These included pottery fragments from the Orientalising period, Attic fragments from the Classical and Hellenistic periods, and fine-glazed Byzantine pottery. Several marble architectural blocks and a number of bronze coins from the Hellenistic age were also found, including one bearing the effigy of Heracles and another of Artemis. Particularly exciting for excavators was the discovery of sculptures including the torso of a warrior, a beautiful stele with a man-at-arms visible against the background, and two sculpted panels from the Imperial era depicting gladiators.

Archaeologists at Thassos have identified three phases in the history of the harbour installations, which must have been built and rebuilt at various times. The fortified walls of the military harbour had been constructed between the end of the 6th century and the beginning of the 5th century BC, as had the mole in the merchant harbour.

Archaeologists were able to glean invaluable information about this type of infrastructure from the extremely well preserved military harbour. The ship sheds were dated to the middle of the 5th century BC. Archaeologists also discovered that the fortified walls were reinforced by circular towers around the 4th century BC, the same period as the construction of the artificial beach. The military harbour was also equipped with ship sheds in its northeastern section and according to ancient texts, Thassos could accommodate up to 50 triremes.

The early Christian period between the 4th and 7th centuries AD brought a number of changes to the military harbour. The entrance was moved, a new section of the sea wall was built and the harbour turned to trading rather than military pursuits. It finally sank into a state of neglect in the 6th century AD, in which it remained until being brought back into service once more in the 10th century.

The reconstruction of a Classical harbour: Piraeus

In order to discourage any attack on Athens from the sea, Themistocles decided to build a harbour that could accommodate its fleet. The chosen site was the rocky peninsula of Piraeus and construction began in 493 BC.

Enclosed by the plain of Akte in the southwest and Munychia hill in the northeast, which were connected by an isthmus, the bays at the Piraeus site offered three ideally protected, natural harbours. The largest of these, called *Megas Limen* or Large Harbour, lay west of the isthmus and became known as Cantharus. To the east, between the plain of Akte and the Munychia hill, was the harbour at Zea, whose entrance formed a 40m wide neck. The small oval-shaped

Aerial view of the port of Piraeus, Athens.

© Yann Arthus-Bertrand/CORBIS

Munychia harbour was situated below the hill of the same name. The project begun by Themistocles in the mid-5th century BC was completed under the successive rules of Cimon and Pericles. The first phase was the construction of the Long Walls, a double wall 10km long, which protected the road connecting the city to the harbour, and the second phase was the construction of the city itself.

Piraeus enjoyed a period of great prosperity during the 5th and 4th centuries BC, when Athens ruled the Aegean Sea and most of its supplies came from the Euxine Sea. During the 3rd century BC, the Macedonian army established itself around the Munychia harbour, which became a naval base for Macedonian conquests in Greece. At the start of the Roman era, in 86 BC, the harbour was destroyed by Sulla.

A large part of the harbour installations was still visible as late as the 19th century. However, the construction of the new harbour and bombardment during the Second World War put paid to further investigations. We do, however, know the layout of ancient Piraeus thanks to detailed descriptions found in many ancient texts and reports from archaeologists who excavated the site in the 19th century, such as E. Dodwell in 1801, W. M Leake in 1821, E. Curtius in 1841, H. N. Ulrichs in 1843 and C. von Strantz in 1861.

Underwater exploration of the harbour was first carried out under the direction of I. Dragatsis in 1885, but more recent excavations were undertaken in 1958-59 by the Greek Ephorate of Underwater Antiquities in the Argolid and Corinth. They specifically targeted the Zea harbour and the Munychia ship sheds.

Cantharus

Cantharus was located to the northwest of the Piraeus peninsula and was the largest natural harbour in the Mediterranean. According to maps produced by archaeologists in the 19th century, it had a roughly rectangular shape and was 1,000m long by 750m wide.

The southern section contained trireme sheds and was used for both military and trading purposes. In the north and east was the *emporion*, a huge esplanade 250m by 1,000m which attracted merchants from throughout the Mediterranean region. They came to display their merchandise and once their cargoes had been inspected, they moored their ships in the bay and transferred their goods to smaller craft or unloaded them on a quayside open to the sea.

The remains of these constructions disappeared in 1840, when they were destroyed to make way for the modern harbour. Archaeological analysis was made easier by the fact that the location and size of each quay was marked by special stones, called *horoi*.

Two moles extended from the harbour walls, narrowing the entrance. These moles were 130m in length and left an entrance 50m wide. This entrance had two towers, linked by a chain, which protected the harbour from sudden attack. Remains of lighthouses were also found at two locations along the coast.

In the northern and eastern sections of the harbour wall were five *stoas*, large

Ship sheds in the eastern section of the port at Zea excavated by Dragatsis and Dörpfeld in 1885.

Photograph attributed to W. Dörpfeld, March 1891

porticos with marble columns. These were used as warehouses for grain from various Greek trading posts and colonies. Another, the *deigma*, acted as the sample market, where Greek and foreign goods destined to be sold in the Emporion were displayed and trading negotiations took place. The nearby quay, known as the *choma*, was reserved for the military ceremonies that were held before major maritime expeditions. Pieces of foundation discovered near one of the porticos suggest the existence of an 80m-long wall.

The Zea harbour

The Danish archaeologist Bjørn Lovén directed the land-based and underwater excavations of the ancient harbour of Zea, Piraeus's second largest harbour. Because of the favourable natural setting, it was built before the two others. The circular basin was 450m in diameter. As with the larger harbour, two moles formed the entrance, each ending in a rectangular tower. The entrance was 200m long by 180m wide and a 50m long wall separated the naval zone from the rest of the city.

This harbour was built for military purposes and most of the warships were moored here, in groups of four or eight, separated by columns supporting sloping tiled roofs. These sheds were extended into the water to enable the triremes to leave more easily. Other similar ruins were found at Oeniadea in western Greece, and at Apollonia in Cyrenaica.

One of the few ancient harbours to provide much information about the ships that used it, Zea has been responsible for a great leap forward in naval archaeology. Records from 326 BC show 360 triremes passed through the Zea harbour. These triremes were roughly 35m long and were crewed by 170 rowers and 20 sailors, all free men, not slaves.

In 347-346 BC, Euvoulus commissioned the architects Philo and Euthydomos to design a new arsenal. A partial excavation of this was begun in 1888. The archaeologists used ancient texts from Plutarch, Strabo and Pliny, as well as an inscription by Philo on a marble block, discovered a century earlier, in 1888, giving details of the construction methods.

Located to the north of the harbour, just behind the ship sheds, the arsenal's architectural beauty was admired by all who saw it. Pliny even compared it to the temple of Artemis in Ephesus. In reality, the arsenal was not used for stocking munitions, but served instead as a warehouse for everything needed to fit out warships. It had been built on a southwest-northeast axis to improve

Model of boat sheds in the port of Zea.

© Hellenic Maritime Museum

ventilation, as Philo attached great importance to the smallest detail.

The walls and base were constructed using marble blocks from quarries on the Akte peninsula. It was 130m long by 18m wide and the gently sloping roof was protected by Corinthian tiles. Apertures high up on the sides let in the light, and slits lower down provided ventilation.

Philo's arsenal was entered through a double portal. The interior consisted of three imposing aisles separated by a double row of columns. The centre aisle served as a public passageway and equipment for the ships was stored in the side aisles, each of which was divided into 34 compartments. Behind each pair of columns, enclosed areas with shelving were used to store ropes and other items. Chests on the floor contained the sails and the rest was stored high up in cupboards. This impressive building was completed in 330 BC.

The Naval Installations at Zea harbour in Piraeus

Bjørn Lovén

The construction of the harbour installations in Piraeus, the harbour city of Athens, was begun on the advice of Themistocles when he became Archon in 493-492 BC. Themistocles was convinced that the future of Athens lay at sea, and that the city needed a large navy and a fortified naval harbour. He also identified Piraeus as the ideal location.

In the 330s BC Zea harbour (also called Pasalimani until recently) had a capacity of 196 warships, and it was Athens's most important naval harbour. The two other harbours in Piraeus, Cantharus (today the large commercial harbour, which was a combined naval and commercial harbour in Antiquity) and the naval harbour Munychia (modern Mikrolimano), housed 94 and 82 warships, respectively.

We know from several ancient sources that ship sheds were built in Piraeus during the 5th century BC, but we do not know in which of the three harbours. In 404 BC, at the end of the Peloponnesian War, Sparta paid the Thirty Tyrants to demolish most of the ship sheds in Piraeus.

Athens once again made a bid for naval dominance in the power struggle that followed the death of Alexander the Great in the summer of 323 BC. In 322 BC, however, the Athenians were defeated in a decisive battle near the island of Amorgos in the southern Cyclades, and the defeat marked the end of Athens's dream of regaining her former status as one of the great naval powers of the Mediterranean.

Sulla sacked Piraeus in 87-86 BC, but according to Pausanias there were still ship sheds there in the 2nd century AD, and the harbours probably functioned as a naval base during the Roman period.

The Zea Harbour Project is a cooperation between the Danish Institute at Athens, the Ephorate of Underwater Antiquities, and the Second Ephorate of Prehistoric and Classical Antiquities.

The lower submerged part of the ship shed. The ruins of the others are visible in the background.

© Christensen K.

In addition, the Hellenic Maritime Museum has kindly granted permission to investigate column drums which in all probability came from the Zea ship sheds and were found in the harbour basin in 1964. The primary objective of the project is to investigate the ship sheds and the submerged parts of the harbour fortifications.

The ship sheds took up most of the available space around the harbour basin. Triremes and other types of warships were hauled out of the water when not operational and stored in ship sheds to protect the hulls from shipworm, sun and rain.

In 1872, Graser carried out the first underwater investigations of what he believed were the submerged parts of ship sheds in Zea and Munychia, and our investigations suggest that his identification of a large number of ship sheds in Zea was correct.

In 1885, Dragatsis and Dörpfeld excavated the remains of 10 ship sheds on land in the eastern part of Zea, and Dragatsis also reported that the remains of the ship sheds continued into the sea. The upper part of three ship sheds excavated by Dragatsis and Dörpfeld are preserved in the basement of the building on the corner of Akti Moutsopoulou and Sirangiou.

In 2001, we investigated the harbour basin in front of the basement so that any findings could be related to the remains on land. We located several architectural structures during the survey, including rock-cut slots for transverse timbers on the slipways, remains of the colonnades, and most importantly the lower end of the ship sheds.

For the first time, we were able to measure the total length of a trireme ship shed at 50.5m. Since no wrecks have been found of ancient Greek warships, the overall dimensions of the ship sheds provide important evidence for the length and width of these vessels.

The harbours of Piraeus were fortified towards both the city and the sea, and we have also found underwater remains of the two fortified quays which made it possible to close the harbour mouth, either with chains or a wooden bar.

In 2002, we excavated modern deposits and completed the 1885 excavation of the ship sheds preserved in the basement.

The objective of this investigation was to expose the ship sheds fully and to investigate whether archaeological deposits which related to construction had been overlooked in the 1885 excavation. We discovered a pit which contained archaeological material from the 4th century BC. We also began to excavate the submerged lower part of the best preserved shed in the basement.

Visibility on shallow water sites is often very poor, and we therefore excavated inside a clear-water enclosure system invented by Mr Charles Pochin. The system consists of a 4m^2 frame of floating plastic tubing, from which a curtain of durable PVC-coated sheeting hangs down, weighted at the bottom by sandbags.

Clear water is pumped into the enclosure from further out in the harbour basin, which helps create the visibility needed to allow precision work underwater. The dirty water and sediment is removed from the enclosure with the dredge used for excavating the architectural structures under water.

The fleet was the basis of Athens's power in the Classical period, and our investigations deal with one of the largest building complexes of classical Greece. In the eastern part of the Zea harbour we estimate that more than 3,000m^2 of the ancient harbour is preserved underwater, and we hope that future exploration will reveal further ancient remains in other parts of the harbour.

The Munychia harbour

This small harbour also contained ship sheds for triremes. Strabo wrote that houses had been built on Munychia hill. Like the harbours of Cantharus and Zea, the one at Munychia also possessed two moles with a tower at each end. The southwest mole was 190m in length and the north-eastern one 95m. A building discovered in the middle of the sea wall may have been a lighthouse or small temple. The Munychia harbour basin was in the form of an ellipse 360m long and 220m wide. Its ship sheds were divided into two 5.3m long parallel compartments.

The fortified walls of Athens

Munychia harbour was completely encircled by fortified walls, completed in 479 BC. The entrance to Piraeus consisted of two large gates, the oldest edifices on the site. They were built using large limestone blocks laid on a foundation of rough brickwork and joined together at the top by metal clamps.

Additional walls were probably constructed at the end of the 5th century BC.

The Long Walls, which stretched from Piraeus to Athens.

© David Lees/CORBIS

One of them skirted the large harbour, following the western coast of the Eetioneia headland as far as the dam known as *Dia mesou choma* and then continuing alongside the harbour to a point south of the Emporion. Another wall, 8m thick, had been built on flat ground more vulnerable to attack between Cantharus and the northeast part of Munychia hill. Finally, the defence of this zone was reinforced by a 10m wide ditch.

In order to consolidate Athens's links with the harbour, in 478 BC Themistocles undertook the construction of the Long Walls mentioned earlier – two rows of parallel walls, with the later addition of a third, which stretched from Piraeus to Athens. These walls guaranteed permanent access to the sea in the event of a siege and allowed weapons and supplies to move freely between the harbour and the city. In wartime, inhabitants of the surrounding areas could take refuge behind them. This unparalleled construction served as a model for other cities, Corinth and Megara in particular.

The great ambition of Themistocles succeeded in making Piraeus an important naval and trading centre, which in turn transformed Athens into an unsurpassed maritime power for at least a century. The strength of the city's fleet enabled the Athenians to repel the Persian invasion and subjugate the rival cities of Aegina and Corinth.

3. Shipwrecks

Transporting goods by sea was popular for economic as well as practical reasons. Ships could carry large quantities over great distances maximising ship owners' profits, despite the ever-present risk of shipwreck. Following developments in underwater archaeology, the wrecks of these ships, lost to storms or broken on rocks, today offer the greatest insight into the maritime and economic history of the Ancient Greek world.

The Helladic cargo of the Dokos wreck

The site on the island of Dokos was discovered in 1975 by the American, Peter Throckmorton, one of the pioneers of underwater archaeology in the late 1950s. He lived in Greece and greatly contributed to the development of underwater archaeology in that country. He also helped to create HIMA (the Hellenic Institute of Marine Archaeology) in 1973, the first national agency devoted to the study and preservation of Greece's underwater heritage.

Dokos is a small island off the southern tip of the Argolic peninsula. In 1975

A diver salvages objects at the site of the Dokos wreck.

© HIMA

and 1977, HIMA undertook two preliminary surveys of the site under the direction of George Papathanassopoulos and followed this up with a full-scale excavation between 1989 and 1992. To call this a wreck was, strictly speaking, a misnomer because nothing actually remained of the ship itself – all biodegradable material such as wood, leather and fabrics had disintegrated. However, the cargo, which included 15,000 pottery shards, two anchors and other artefacts gave archaeologists enough information to suggest a date and origin for the ship and helped them build a fuller picture of the level of trade occurring during the first Bronze Age.

The pottery dated the wreck to 2200 BC, making it the oldest ever found. At that time in history, the power of the Cyclades was beginning to wane and would soon be supplanted by the Cretan civilisation.

Doctor Yannis Vichos describes some of the various techniques used during the underwater archaeological excavation of the site.

First year of the Dokos wreck excavation

Yannis Vichos

Preliminary surveys of the underwater site in 1975 and 1977 had revealed the difficulties that a systematic archaeological exploration would entail. Although the maximum depth of the archaeological field did not exceed 32m, it was clear, given the steep incline of the ocean floor and the large number of artefacts, that the length of time required to lay out a traditional grid and locate artefacts using any known topographical technique would make it unwise to undertake such a project.

A detailed survey was carried out three months before the start of the first excavation proper by HIMA, under the direction of G. Papathanassopoulos. Using a portable probe, we were able to draw up a chart of the sea floor, which confirmed our earlier findings and influenced our choice of an appropriate method and the systems required to implement it.

Having discarded the traditional grid plan and topographical survey, we turned towards a completely new underwater cartography system, SHARPS (Sonic High Accuracy Recording and Positioning System), developed by technicians at INA (the Institute of Nautical Archeology). This system uses high-frequency sound waves to locate objects – on a two-dimensional plane and in terms of depth – and records the data directly on to a computer.

Since the use of SHARPS at Dokos in 1989 was a world first, we decided to back up the topographical survey with comprehensive stereophotographic cover. This was achieved using a camera moving along a grid pattern of metal tubes, taking pictures at regular intervals with a minimum overlap rate of 60%. After stereoscopic processing of the images, it was possible to obtain a photogrammetric topographical map.

The decision to employ two different topographical systems, both of which actually met the same requirements, was a deliberate one, intended to

The excavation site was strewn with pottery and amphorae.

© HIMA

A diver inspects the remains of an amphora.

© HIMA

produce more accurate results through a comparison of the two sets of data. Once the excavation's most difficult problem – that of the topographical survey – had been solved, we still had to complete the remaining objectives for this initial campaign: marking out the zone to be explored, locating artefacts in the upper layers, placing numbered labels for each item or group of items, removing all visible artefacts and transferring them to a safe place in a museum.

The task of marking out the zone to be explored was entrusted to two archaeological divers who were also responsible for locating the artefacts.

These were marked by plastic labels with white numbers on a black background. In view of the quantity of finds, the labels were used to indicate groups of artefacts rather than individual items.

Artefacts were then placed in plastic bags marked with their assigned number and brought to the surface in groups. The plastic bags containing the artefacts were transported in buckets and basins filled with water. Every effort was made to conduct an exemplary excavation in terms of methodology, not only by employing the most advanced technology, but also by recording meticulously every detail about the site.

Exploration report

Once the equipment had been transported and the land and sea installations set up, a number of underwater surveys were carried out confirming that most of the finds lay at a depth of between 15m and 32m, over a surface area of 690m^2, which was then marked out by ropes attached to 18 numbered metal stakes. This zone was surveyed using both the traditional method and SHARPS. When data collated by the two methods were compared, SHARPS proved to be completely reliable, as well as considerably faster. The area to be explored was then subdivided into nine sections.

After the installation of SHARPS, which took a week, the divers, who worked in pairs, began the task of locating artefacts and groups of artefacts using labels numbered from A1 to A250 (the letter A denoting the top layer). They then recorded the numbers, completed a brief description and photographed the artefacts *in situ*, noting their position using SHARPS.

The SHARPS positioning was carried out by a diver linked to the surface, pointing a kind of sound-emitting pistol at the relevant label. The position was then relayed back to a computer operator in the surface vessel.

At the same time, we began the stereophotographic survey of sections

Artefacts were found buried amid rocks and concretions.

© HIMA

Divers label the artefacts and the remains of the cargo prior to marking them on a site map.

© HIMA

that were particularly rich in material, though not before undertaking a preliminary superficial clean-up.

During this, we discovered two large slabs of greenish schist pierced with a hole and lying at a depth of about 34m and 38m, respectively, 14m from the site of the wreck. The odds are that these slabs, weighing 18,500kg and 21,500kg, are ancient anchors directly connected with the wreck.

We then moved on to the cartographical survey of the area being explored using SHARPS and recalculated the position of the archaeological field in relation to the coastline, so that we could transfer it to the topographical map.

The next stage involved systematically putting the finds in labelled plastic bags and bringing them to the surface, section by section. Bags from the same section were placed in a metal basket attached to a balloon which was inflated to raise the basket to the floating platform. The mission director, G. Papathanassopoulos, and other archaeologists began an initial recording of the finds, which they placed with their bags and labels in buckets of seawater.

All the work was photographed and partially filmed and, on the final day, the finds were transported to the archaeological museum on Spetses.

Exploration findings

Most of the finds lay within the marked-off area. The irregular layout of the sections did not hamper surveying operations as the SHARPS system works independently of any grid, on an imaginary horizontal plane determined by three fixed wavelength receivers. The nine original sections, which have to be further subdivided to facilitate the work, were used exclusively for locating, surveying and collecting the finds.

The 1989 campaign yielded unexpected results in terms of the site's cartography and the survey of locations. The methods chosen proved totally satisfactory, their application created few problems on the whole, and the decision to use two rival surveying systems turned out to be an eminently sensible means of compensating for the inevitable shortcomings of either system.

Although the data is still being processed, the AutoCAD programme has already provided us with a complete map of the area explored, giving the location of all finds as well as their hypsometry.

At the end of the 1989 campaign, all the visible finds were brought to the surface. The process of recording these as soon as they came out of the water proved particularly useful and should be carried out even more systematically in the future.

Of the 1,381 objects recorded, most were vase fragments dating, for the most part, from the end of the Early Helladic II (the term Helladic comes from the first Bronze Age, 2500-2000 BC).

II. Thalassa, the Greek sea

Early Helladic II-type ceramics

The cargo lay littered along a sloping bank which descended to a depth of 32m. Pottery found amongst the cargo included all known examples of Early Helladic II, typical pottery for this period, of which archaeologists had already found some examples in land sites. Saucers, deep and medium-depth bowls, pots, jugs and plates were found amongst the artefacts. The many pots found belonged to the Askitario typological class. Identifying the origin of these vases was to be one of the notable results of this study. The team also retrieved fragments of a *pyxis*, a cylindrical or spherical box with a lid.

Among the larger vases, several wide-lipped earthenware jars, an amphora and a *pithos* were of particular note. The *pithos*, which was half buried, was a large jar which would have been used for stocking and transporting flour or oil.

The ship was also carrying several *askoi*, a sort of flat pitcher with a horizontal neck and basket-like handle, resembling a primitive wineskin. Other objects were raised which are still in use today, in particular a cooking plate and a candleholder. The rest of the cargo was made up of grinding wheels, fragments of lead ingots, from the mines at Laurion, obsidian blade shafts and two anchors made from schist rock.

The abundance of coins found suggests that the ship must have been fairly large. However, this hypothesis was proved unfounded by the discovery of two

Remains of an amphora found at the Dokos site.

© HIMA, photo: K. Xenikakis

anchors, whose modest weight and size meant that they could only have been designed for a boat of between 15m and 20m long.

Stone anchors

It is always difficult to attribute a precise date to ancient anchors, as their characteristics evolved slowly over centuries. As one would expect, those found at the Dokos site demonstrated all the qualities one would expect from an anchor of the early Bronze Age. The pair lay only 14m from the cargo and were embedded in a stony seabed. The first, which was triangular, lay 34m down, quite close to the bank. The other was more rounded and lay at 38m. They each had a hole at one end. Both anchors were photographed *in situ* and their positions fixed by measuring their distances from different points on the perimeter of the main site and from each other.

To be certain of where the anchors had come from, the archaeologists passed a rope through the ancient holes and tried to raise them from the base boat above the wreck site. This required a lot of effort, so they moved the boat to right above the anchors and tried again. This time it required less exertion to move the slabs. This experiment, together with the distances of the anchors from the cargo site and their positions to the west of it, are consistent with their having belonged to the Dokos wreck. For if the vessel were anchored in the approximate position of the wreck site and were caught by a strong westerly wind (the most dangerous in the bay of Skindos), and if it had then broken up on the

Divers prise artefacts from the site of the wreck at Point Iria using a sediment cleaner.

© HIMA

A stirrup jar half-buried in the sea floor.
© HIMA

rocky shore and sank, its anchors would have been left in just these positions.

The other artefacts found at the site, typical of the Argolid regions and central and continental Greece, led researchers to believe that the Dokos ship had been on a regular, short voyage. The wreck site was on the maritime trade route joining the southern Euboean Bay to the Saronic and the Argolic Gulfs, with the large protohellenic centre of Lerna, so it is likely that the ship came from Attica or Evia and was bound for the Argolic Gulf. The island of Dokos must therefore have been a stopover.

Point Iria: a Bronze Age cargo

Yannos G. Lolos

In 1962, on the seabed off Point Iria about halfway between the Homeric towns of Asine and Mases in the Argolic Gulf, Nikos Tsouchlos located the pottery cargo of a wrecked vessel.

His attention was particularly attracted by a large intact jar (*pithos*) and several pots and fragments half-buried in the sand. The chief concentration of pottery finds lay on a slope with rocks, concretions and small sandy patches, 15m from the rocky shore and some 100m northwest of the tip of Point Iria, at a depth ranging from 12m to 27m.

Although he had come across many wrecked cargoes whilst diving in these waters, there was something about these pots which inspired Nikos to return to the site and investigate further the story of how they had found their resting place here.

Three decades later, systematic excavation carried out by HIMA revealed that the seabed concealed the cargo of a shipwreck from around 1200 BC.

The freight consisted of Cypriot, Cretan and Helladic (Mycenaean)

Selection of amphorae and pottery found at the Point Iria site, and, on the right, one of the ship's anchors.

© HIMA

pottery, offering tangible evidence for maritime trade and contact between Cyprus and the Argolid, and throwing new light on facets of Cypro-Mycenaean relations at the very end of the 13th century BC, around the time of the Trojan War.

In September 1998, 36 years after his discovery in the Gulf of Argos, Nikos Tsouchlos, in his address to an international conference on the Point Iria wreck on the island of Spetses, used the following words to describe the first reconnaissance of the wreck site and certainly one of the finest hours in his long career as an underwater explorer:

"By the 1960s I was a fairly experienced scuba diver and in my underwater excursions I very often came across ancient finds, either scattered or in concentrations, the probable remains of shipwrecks. This was how, some 30 years ago, in one of my dives I happened on the Iria wreck. But this time, unlike in the past, it aroused a strong interest in me. It might have been the large size of the pots, or possibly their completely different shapes; perhaps also it was the culmination of my interest in our nautical history.

"This time I didn't see them as isolated lifeless objects; I felt I was looking at the living evidence of the last tragic moments of a ship and its crew. The Iria wreck was the cause of a change in my approach, which took me down a new road and in a certain way determined my future course."

Following further reconnaissance of the wreck site in 1971, 1974 and 1990, the investigation of the 32 centuries old shipwreck, achieved in the course of four successive seasons and largely sponsored by the A. G. Leventis Foundation and INSTAP (the Institute for Aegean Prehistory), was HIMA's second large-scale underwater research project (the first had been at Dokos, in the Aegean, discussed above).

HIMA assembled a large and efficient team, comprising archaeologists, students, technicians, preservation experts and other personnel, who successfully completed the excavation of the wreck. In all over 80 people were involved in the operations. In June 1993 a fully organised camp, serving as the team's base, was set up on land by Nikos Tsouchlos, Yannis Baltsavias and Petros Vakondios on the Iria beach, at some distance north of the wreck site.

This camp was later to be visited by such distinguished archaeologists and researchers as H. Frost, P. Pomey, A. J. Parker, Sp. Iakovidis, V. Karageorghis, Ch. Kritzas and A. Kyrou, as news spread fast about the age and identity of the wreck.

It was a wreck belonging to the Late Bronze Age, only the third of this size to have been found and excavated in the cosmopolitan eastern Mediterranean world, after the more famous ones at Cape Gelidonya and Uluburun on the south coast of Anatolia. This wreck represented an invaluable source of evidence for the study of long-distance barter trade at the time.

The archaeologists, having realised the wider implications of the find, succeeded in completing the conservation, full study and exhibition of the wrecked cargo in 1998, only four years after the close of the work on the seabed.

Those were happy days for us all and for me personally at the wreck site and at the base camp, under the heavy shadow of the trees on the shore.

As I write these lines, as a memorial to Nikos, almost 10 years after the close of the 1994 campaign, I vividly remember his euphoria at the outset of the project – instilled into all the members of the team – after the recognition of the Cypriot origin of a heavy broad-based water jug (jug A20 or 'the Tsouchlos jug').

This jug, now on exhibition in the museum of Spetses, might well have belonged to members of the ship's crew. Nikos, diving at the wreck site with George Masselos, raised it from the seabed on 26 September 1971, and kept it safely in his house at Athens for almost two decades. Thought to be Geometric or Archaic at that time, it was finally handed over to the Spetses museum upon the initiation of the Institute's Point Iria Project.

Regrettably, the large intact *pithos*, which had first caught the eye of Nikos on the seabed at Point Iria back in 1962 and inspired him, was stolen in the long period that elapsed between the 1974 filming of the wreck by Bruno Vailati and the beginning of the systematic excavation by the Institute.

Our only record now of that large Cypriot container from the Point Iria wreck is an excellent colour photograph of the find taken by Nikos, as he was writing, in the Gulf of Argos, the history of underwater archaeology in Greece.

Master seafarers

II. Thalassa, *the Greek sea*

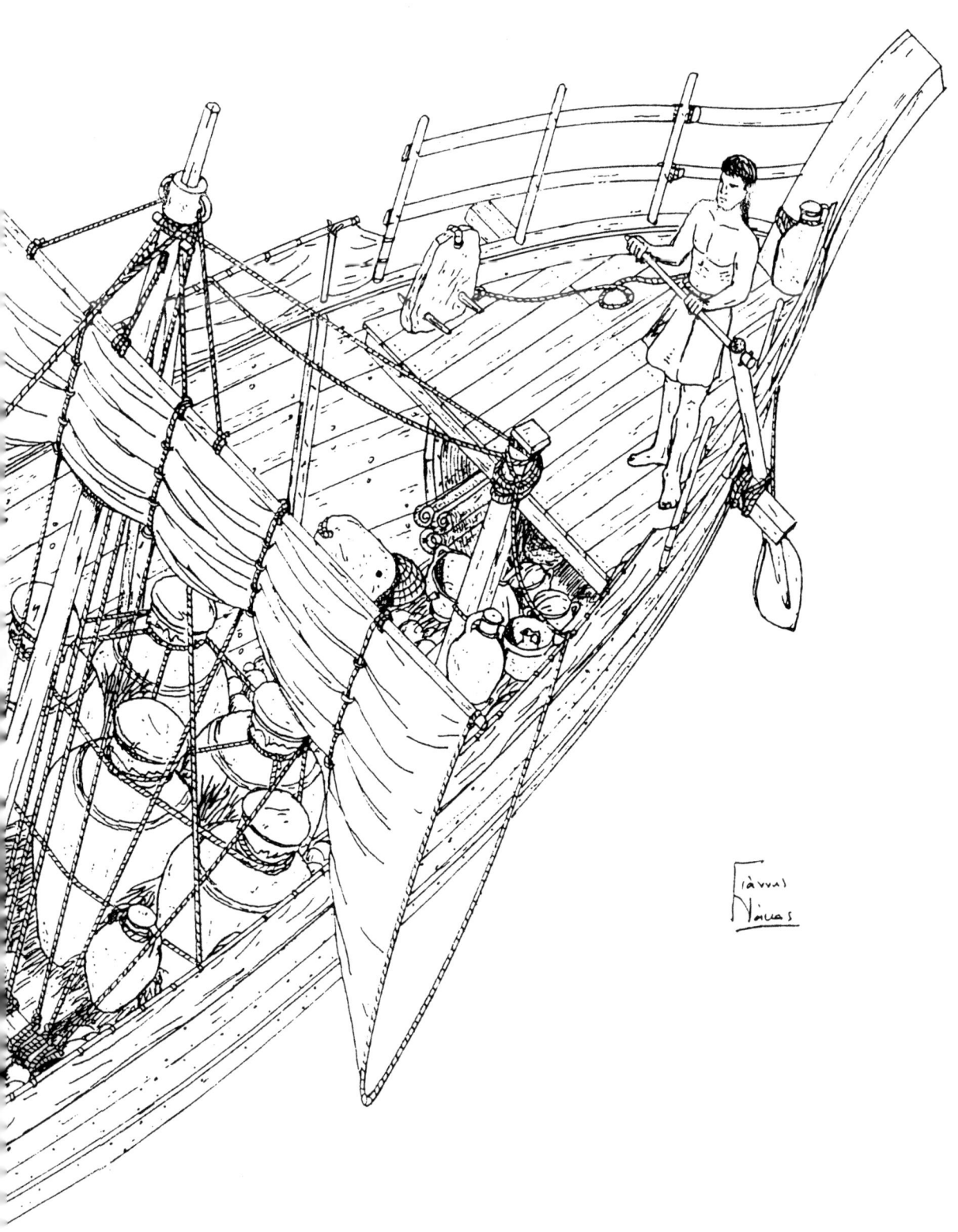

A reconstruction of the Point Iria wreck.

© HIMA, drawing: Yannis Nakas

The Point Iria wreck

Yannos G. Lolos

This wreck, dating from around 1200 BC, lay off Point Iria on the south coast of the Argolid in southern Greece. It was discovered by the late Nikos Tsouchlos, one of the founding fathers of underwater archaeology in Greece, in 1962. Its systematic excavation, orchestrated by Tsouchlos, was conducted by Athens-based HIMA (the Hellenic Institute of Marine Archaeology), between 1991 and 1994, under the direction of Charalambos Pennas and Yannis Vichos. The wreck has become widely known after the opening of the permanent exhibition of its cargo in the museum of Spetses in 1998 and the publication of the proceedings of a special conference held on the island of Spetses, in the following year.

This wreck is possibly that of a Cypriot-based merchant boat travelling in Aegean waters, no more than 10m long and built by the 'shell-first' technique. It carried (like most ancient wrecks) a cargo of mixed ceramics, made up of Cypriot, Cretan and Helladic/Mycenaean pottery, that can be contrasted with the predominantly metallic cargo of the contemporary Cape Gelidonya wreck on the south coast of Anatolia.

The Point Iria wreck represents a valuable piece of evidence for Cypro-Argive contacts in the late 13th and early 12th century BC, already highlighted in several studies. A ring of coastal towns (Tiryns, Nauplion, Asine) and a local network of island stations are likely to have played an important role in this exchange.

Despite its limited size, the cargo of pottery from the Point Iria wreck is one of the very few cargoes of ceramics that has so far been retrieved from the wreck of a Late Bronze Age merchant ship in the Mediterranean, and casts fresh light on the character and content of long-distance maritime trade around 1200 BC.

The cargo contains 25 pots, in addition to an intact Cypriot *pithos* (large jar), which is now unfortunately lost. These pots seem to have formed the main bulk of the ship's cargo, but perhaps not the whole of it and comprise three main groups of pottery: Late Cypriot IIC/IIIA; Late Minoan (Cretan) III B2; and a Late Helladic (Mycenaean) III B2 group of nine vases. All three groups are found in the cargo of large transport vessels.

Prominent in the first group are well fired Cypriot *pithoi*, which had various functions. The second consists of coarse-ware stirrup jars (false-necked jars) of Cretan provenance, known as *chlareis* in the Linear B texts of Knossos and Pylos, and intended primarily for storing and transporting olive oil and wine. With regard to their manufacture, the eight stirrup jars on the Point Iria wreck form, on the whole, a homogeneous group, with an origin in central Crete, and therefore might represent a tightly composed shipment intended perhaps for some centre in the Argolid. The third group is dominated by three large two-handled jars of Late Helladic type, with close Peloponnesian parallels.

Photograph of the cargo of the wreck in an exhibition in the museum at Spetses, in Greece.

© HIMA, photo: K. Xenikakis

The Cypriot *pithos* – with an ovoid or ovoid-conical body and often carrying multiple relief bands – and the tall Aegean stirrup jar are established ceramic types, and were distributed throughout the ancient world during the late 14th and 13th century BC. They have appeared as far afield as Ugarit in Syria, Cyprus and Agrigento in southern Sicily and Antigori in southern Sardinia.

The distribution of the ceramic cargo of the Point Iria wreck, established by the combined presence of Cypriot and Aegean ceramic types, has obvious parallels in the large cargo of pottery from the Uluburun wreck, of circa 1300 BC, and to some extent in that of the Cape Gelidonya wreck of circa 1200 BC.

Completely absent from the extant ceramic material on the Point Iria wreck are Syro-Palestinian wares, such as small vessels for everyday use and Canaanite jars. The coexistence and contemporary circulation of Aegean, Cypriot and even Syro-Palestinian wares is not out of place at major ports in the 14th and 13th centuries BC, like Tiryns, Chania (Kydonia) and Kommos on the south coast of Crete.

The character of the ceramic content of the Point Iria wreck should be viewed as a reflection of a typical circulation pattern of specific types of transport vessels and commodities, within the context of long distance barter trade in the eastern and central Mediterranean around 1200 BC.

A diver lifts an amphora from its resting place on the seabed.
© HIMA

On the evidence of the material raised from the seabed, a Cypriot rather than a Mycenaean origin for the Point Iria ship can perhaps be surmised. Large Cypriot *pithoi* – which would have served as permanent onboard containers – are present, as well as three Cypriot jugs, probably belonging to the ship's crew, and also incised merchants' marks (made after firing) have been identified on the handles of a Mycenaean type amphora, closely matched on pots from Minet-el-Beida in Syria and on Cypriot copper ingots from the cargo of the Uluburun wreck, and arguably related to the Cypro-Minoan I Script.

Far from the case of the exceptional 'royal' cargo of the Uluburun wreck, the wrecked cargo on the seabed at Point Iria is rather unlikely to have been a special shipment commissioned by some central authority. Yet, in the context of trading and shipping in the years around 1200 BC, it is a very safe indicator of regular sea traffic on the route from Cyprus to the Argolid, perhaps via Crete or other islands.

The Alonnisos wreck

The island of Ikos (modern day Alonnisos), in the north of the Aegean Sea, remained under Athenian rule until the time of the Delean League. Like all the islands of the Northern Sporades, it was a convenient stop-off for Athenian ships bound for Mende in the northern Aegean, the Euxine Sea and Chios. The large number of wrecks recovered off these islands suggests that the maritime traffic in the region must have been extremely heavy, yet very few of them have been excavated or documented.

One of the most important was discovered in 1985 off the coast of Alonnisos by a Greek fisherman, and has been the subject of an extensive series of dives. These began in 1992 under the direction of E. Hadjidaki, with an initial programme of photogrammetry, designed to produce maps and plans for the excavation. In 1993, a grid system was laid out, a study made of the artefacts, photographs taken and detailed drawings made of the cargo.

The Alonnisos wreck measures approximately 30m long by 10m wide. The wreck's cargo, spread across an incline at between 22 and 33m, comprised high quality black-glazed pottery, the best of which came from Athens, and a cargo of more than 4,000 perfectly preserved wine amphorae.

The wine amphorae had been made in Mende and on the islands of Ikos and Peparethos (modern day Skopelos) between 420 BC and 400 BC. While Mende produced a wine celebrated for its quality throughout the region, the wine from Peparethos, according to the Athenians, was second rate. This did not stop Athenian merchants from buying it to distribute in the Aegean and around the Euxine Sea.

The Mendean amphorae were different to those from Peparethos because of their rounded shape. They were light red and 61cm high by 38cm at the widest point. The Peparethian amphorae were more elongated. They had long necks and rounded shoulders, and were 76–81cm high and 32cm at the widest point. They are also known as Solocha II amphorae and many of this type have been found around the Euxine and the Aegean Seas.

The excavation uncovered items of crockery in such quantity that they could not have belonged to the ship, but must have been part of the cargo. These included heavy terracotta mortars with two handles, a large base and a thick, rounded lip. There were also *skyphoi* – goblets with two horizontal handles. They were both partly glazed in black and beautifully decorated on the interior with palmettes, and may well have come from Athens. Also found were black-glazed Athenian cups with concave necks and petals engraved on the body, several Athenian drinking vessels, with interiors finely decorated with concentric circles with stars at the centre, bowls with black-glazed bases, which seem to have come from southern Italy, as well as an Athenian oil lamp.

Other items probably belonged to the crew. Among the utensils found were: an elegant pitcher with a large annulated body; a *chytra*, a receptacle for serving hot water; and a number of metal objects, which included a slightly eroded bronze *kados* with a bell-shaped body. These elegant vessels were used for carrying wine and water. The team also found two lead cross-bars from an anchor.

A study of the cargo dated the wreck to around 415 BC, a time when the Athenians controlled sea trade from the Mediterranean to the Euxine Sea.

From Ikos to Peparethos

The location and content of the cargo give us a good idea of the route the ship was taking. The Athenian crockery, stowed in the ship's hull, indicates that Athens was the first port of call. Above these bowls were Mendean amphorae; and higher still, amphorae from Peparethos. After leaving Athens, the ship must have visited these two ports. It would then have headed for Ikos, which must have been its homeport.

Cargo overload?

As with every wreck, archaeologists wanted to discover why the ship sank. The sea is calm around Ikos and the island's coasts unthreatening. The idea of a natural accident was therefore ruled out. So why did the ship go down?

An analysis of the bowls showed the presence of carbon, indicating that the ship had burnt, so fire must have caused the wreck. Did the Spartans start the fire? Between 420 and 400 BC, the date of the wreck, the Peloponnesian war was at its height. Sparta was attacking towns in the northern Aegean, and Mende in particular, but there is no literary source to indicate that this conflict extended to the Sporades islands.

Could it therefore have been a pirate attack? Again, this is by no means certain, although attacks by pirates were commonplace in the 5th century BC, and piracy was particularly bad in the Sporades as the Athenian fleet was no longer powerful enough to police the seas.

Perhaps the real reason the ship sank is simply because it was overloaded. This wreck is the first ship found with a cargo capacity of 120 tonnes, a load which would have been exceptional at this time. The ship's ambitious owners may have been tempted to test its limits, with disastrous results.

The excavation is ongoing and many years will be needed to uncover all the artefacts the Alonnisos ship contains, learn how it was constructed and determine all its ports of call.

The evolution of pottery through the ages

Greek vases were meant above all to be practical, for everyday use. Yet until the Classical Era, ceramics, like all art forms, was subject to continual aesthetic development. This is because for the Greek artisan – in the widest possible meaning of the word – there was no real cut-off point between beauty and practicality, any more than there was, until the 5th century, any significant difference in Greece between an artisan and an artist. Even the simplest pottery is therefore rarely without some artistic value.

As we have a large selection available to us of many different shapes, sizes, styles and decorations, researchers have been able to establish a reliable chronology of ceramic production. These findings in turn help archaeologists to better assess the ancient Greek sites they excavate, which nearly always include some pottery. Wreck sites abound in pottery. Because pots made up a large part of commercially tradable goods, every wreck, on close examination, contains at least some small fragment of vase buried beneath the sand or under a thick layer of algae. It only remains to study these and the history of the sunken ship is revealed.

Cretan and Mycenaean pottery

Terracotta stirrup jar, decorated with serpentine motif. This vase, dating from the Late Minoan III, between the 14th and 13th centuries BC, was discovered in Syria, at Minet el-Beida.

© photo RMN: Franck Raux

From the 2nd millennium to 1400 BC, ceramics from the continent followed the Minoan aesthetic. Largely based on polychromy, this was extremely popular between the 17th and 15th centuries BC. Long before the golden age of Crete, Minoan artists showed a strong preference for incandescent decoration. The 'flame' ceramics of the 3rd millennium relied on a combination of vibrant and subtle marks, ranging from yellow ochre to dark red. This fashion continued after the Middle Minoan III period (i.e. after 1750 BC), when the famous 'Camara' jars, named after a cave in central Crete, were produced.

The principle of ornamentation was based on the contrast of colours. White, yellow, orange and red motifs, both figurative and abstract, jumped out from the vase's dark background. The abstract included swirls, arrows and spirals; the figurative included plants or marine life, often shellfish, algae and jellyfish, whose curves blended to produce a beautiful effect of harmony and movement.

Painting became less popular at this time, as artists turned for new inspiration to metals like gold, silver and bronze. This produced stunning vases with black backgrounds and polished surfaces, producing blue and violet metallic reflections. Technology also advanced, with the invention of the potter's wheel leading to the production of more elegant and ambitious vases with extremely fine walls.

From Late Minoan II (around 1450 BC), this vivid, lively pottery was replaced by something more sombre and less colourful. Brown or black glazes alone embellished the light clay background. The shapes, while still naturalist, were treated with more rigour and discipline. Tentacles lost some of their suppleness, for instance, and leaves were placed symmetrically along stems. Crete had ceased to be the driving force in the Aegean world and would in future be influenced by the mainland, where the Mycenaeans were becoming increasingly powerful.

The influence in the Late Helladic III period, from 1400 BC, was graphical and disciplined. Marine and floral decoration became more and more stylised, bordered by horizontal and vertical lines. In a small number of

II. Thalassa, *the Greek sea*

Painted terracotta water vase, decorated with an octopus, 1200-1100 BC, from the Mycenaean period, Late Helladic III.

© photo RMN: H. Lewandowski

workshops, decoration evolved towards a representation of animals (for example goats, bulls and bears) and even humans. At this time human figures appeared stiff, opaquely silhouetted without any added colour.

The Late Helladic III C (from 1200 BC), saw the Dorian invasion, the decline of Mycenaean civilisation and the impoverishment of the arts. In pottery, this was a period of reduction in form and the extreme simplification of patterns, which were reduced to circles, rosettes or highly stylised animals. Sub-Mycenaean pottery (1150-1000 BC) is marked by an even further decline — undulating waves and poorly hand-drawn circles, in some ways prefiguring the geometric style.

Geometric period

During the phase known as Protogeometric, which lasted until the 10th century BC, there was a rebirth of high standards of drawing and a search for balance and clarity. Artisans returned to themes inherited from the previous era, but now drew them using compasses. The more harmonious decoration was made up of alternating dark and light horizontal stripes. Symbols, although few and far between in this style of decoration, were given a prominent position where they did appear. The shape and structure of vases also became more balanced. Amphorae with two symmetrical necks, separating the surface of the vase in two and so breaking up the pictorial space, replaced earlier vases with three necks.

In the 9th century BC – at the height of the Geometric period, which was dominated by austerity and elegance – new patterns came to enrich decorations. As well as the circles and half circles, we see the dotted line, the arrow, the swastika, the oval and the zigzag, which became the main symbol of Hellenic art. It is also at this time that the traditional forms of vases, particularly amphorae, *hydria*, *kraters*, drinking cups and *pyxides*, took definitive shape. Several particularly refined vases were created, such as the *oenochoe*, a wine pitcher with a three-pronged spout.

Geometric *oenochoe* from Thebes dating from the Recent Geometric period, around 715-700 BC.

© photo RMN: H. Lewandowski

Detail from the *oenochoe* opposite showing two wrestlers.

© photo RMN: H. Lewandowski

From the Middle Geometric period, around 850 BC, most of the vase's surface was being covered in decoration. The theme was still of contrasting dark and light areas, but the decorative stripes were more numerous and contained more symbols. This period saw a gradual return to figurative representation, particularly in Athens, although these differed totally from Mycenaean and Minoan representations in their themes, the way they were treated and their mood. The vases portray weeping women and warriors, funeral scenes depicting the corpse and the procession, lines of chariots and sea battles. The figures

Ancient geometric *pyxide-krater*, from about 800 BC. Geometric shapes and animals are visible.

© photo RMN: H. Lewandowski

stand out from the background, which is often decorated with small motifs. They are rigid and drawn in a diagrammatic way: the head is a circle, the body a triangle and the limbs are stick-like. The arms of the weeping women form rectangles. In these stylised drawings, which suggest more than is represented, no unnecessary detail is included that could trouble the harmony of the composition. The style is dry and minimalist. Decoration is no longer purely ornamental, for the first time it is used to mark important events.

During the Late Geometric period, between 750 and 700 BC, the tendency was towards a surfeit of decoration and the use of multiple ornate areas and the composition therefore lost its rigour and simplicity. The introduction of narrative scenes (for example hunts, armed battles and scenes from mythology), shows the beginning of realist observation and an attention to detail which contrasts to the attitude and language of the Geometric period, which was suggestive rather than descriptive. This period therefore heralds the end of the Geometric style — which didn't last beyond the 7th century outside a small number of workshops — and paved the way for the main 'realist' themes of the Archaic era.

Early Archaic and Orientalising periods

In the 7th century BC, Greece entered into a period of fervent creativity, in large part due to the Near East, with which trade had been re-established. Influenced by Egypt and the Levant, Greek artists renounced the austerity of their predecessors and embraced a new world of fantastic and non-human themes. Images of curving palm leaves, roses and lotus petals replaced the linear illustrations of the Geometric period.

Multicoloured vases were decorated with oriental landscapes of panthers and lions, fantastic scenes with winged horses, sphinx and griffins, and exotic plants. Figurative decoration became more and more detailed, highlighted by incisions engraved with a chisel. The Greeks also copied new types of vases from the Near East, like perfume phials — *aryballos* and *alabastra* — which Greek workshops, particularly in Corinth, began to mass-produce.

Middle and Recent Archaic periods

The taste for the oriental continued into the middle of the 6th century BC, when Greek artists abandoned animals and monsters to concentrate exclusively on the human figure. Scenes either had a certain theme or genre (for instance banquets, ceremonial dances or departing warriors) or epic scenes focusing on heroes such as Theseus and Hercules.

The drawings, at first clumsy and a little rigid, grew more and more skilful and movement eventually became far more free and natural. It was also at the beginning of the 6th century that the use of black-figure technique came into vogue. Black silhouettes were drawn against the terracotta background of the pot with a slip (watered-down clay) that turned black during firing. Details were added with engraved purple or white highlights. The shape of vases also evolved.

Human-shaped impasto pitcher decorated in the geometric style, dating from 710-670 BC from the Orientalising period (Archaic III), found in Etruria.

© photo RMN: H. Lewandowski

In Attica for example, the body of bulbous amphorae became more rounded and a new type of large amphora developed, with a neck and wooden handles.

Around 530 BC, there was a decisive revolution in ceramic art. The invention of the red-figure technique gave artists much greater freedom of expression and initiated the golden age of Greek ceramics, which would last until 480 BC. From now on, the background was picked out in black slip, leaving the decorative motifs the colour of the clay behind. The lightness of the clay gave the painter the ability to portray the human body with a much greater level of detail. Having sketched the outline and the major features of the figures, he circled them with a thick band of paint, then added in the subject's details using a slip and fine pincers.

Black-figure *stamnos*, dating from 510-500 BC, Middle and Recent Archaic periods. The shoulder is decorated with banquet scenes; in the middle, wrestlers and boxers; below, a chariot race.

© photo RMN: H. Lewandowski

The Athenian workshops excelled at this technique and passed it on to others throughout the country. The quality of their glazes was also very high, acquiring a metallic sheen and a deep black, almost blue tint, which typifies Athenian pottery of the 6th and 5th centuries BC. As for the shape of the vases, the bowl, often decorated with fearsome eyes, was extremely successful in Hellenic workshops.

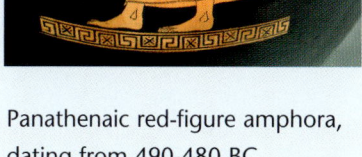

Panathenaic red-figure amphora, dating from 490-480 BC.

© photo: RMN: Ch. Larrieu

Classical and Hellenistic periods

The art of ceramics underwent a decline during the Classical period. Although the range of colours expanded, the quality of the drawing and of the figures became increasingly basic. This was the period of mannerism or 'fine style', dominated by genre painting.

During the Hellenistic period, at the end of the 4th century BC, red figure ceramics disappeared and were soon replaced by figurative decoration, where minimal floral motifs were highlighted against the background of the vase.

Campanian amphora representing Medea killing her son, from the Hellenistic period, around 340-300 BC.

© photo RMN: Chuzeville

There were so many communities in Greece manufacturing pottery that it is impossible to detail the evolution of each one here. None of them produced the same sort of vase at the same time, of course. On the contrary, periods and styles were constantly developing. Corinth manufactured Geometric vases until the 7th century, eastern Greece continued in the Orientalising style at the time when black figures were being produced in Athens, and so on. Furthermore, each school had its own favourite style and type of vase, so there are an infinite number of varieties throughout the evolution of ceramics.

Master seafarers

The Tektas Burnu wreck

This wreck was found in 1996 by INA, between the Greek islands of Chios and Samos, off Tektas Burnu, on Turkey's west coast. The Tektas Burnu vessel, like the Alonnisos wreck, dates back to the end of the 5th century BC, the golden age of Ancient Greece.

The first season of excavation focused on preparing the site: cleaning, clearing objects of any concretions, and noting their locations on maps.

Tektas Burnu

Deborah N. Carlson

In 1996, a survey team from INA (the Institute of Nautical Archeology) located the remains of a Classical Greek shipwreck off the Aegean coast of Turkey at the site of Tektas Burnu. The excavation of the wreck, supervised by George Bass (as director), and myself (assistant director), was carried out by a multinational team over three summers between 1999 and 2001.

The ship, which is believed to have sunk between 440 and 425 BC, constitutes rare and important evidence of small-scale regional trade during the Athenian Empire.

Tektas Burnu, which is Turkish for 'Cape of the Lone Rock', lies southwest of ancient Teos and due east of the Greek island of Chios along a rugged and remote stretch of coastline that is accessible only by sea. During the summer months, the site is exposed to the prevailing northwesterly winds, known as the *meltem*, which routinely produce rough seas and occasionally reach gale force. In the 5th century BC, this coast was part of Ionia, a fertile region of Asia Minor that had successively come under the control of the Lydians, the Persians, and, most recently, the Athenians.

The shipwreck lay on a small shelf at a depth of between 38m and 43m. Good visibility and ample ambient light made it possible to implement a novel mapping system that used photogrammetry by digital camera to produce a three-dimensional site plan. Excavators also had the option of taking traditional direct measurements to quickly record the position of fragile or otherwise at-risk artefacts.

Excavation revealed that this was a small ship, perhaps not more than 10m-12m long, carrying a cargo of wine and pine tar. The largest portion of the cargo consisted of just over 200 pseudo-Samian amphorae, a type that is presently unattributed, but resembles amphorae produced on Samos. One pseudo-Samian amphora carried a stamp that suggests these jars may have been products of the nearby Ionian city of Erythrae. Nine Mendean amphorae from the wreck were filled with pine tar that was still viscous after nearly 2,500 years beneath the waves. Beef ribs had been packed inside one Mendean and one pseudo-Samian amphora. The remainder of the amphora

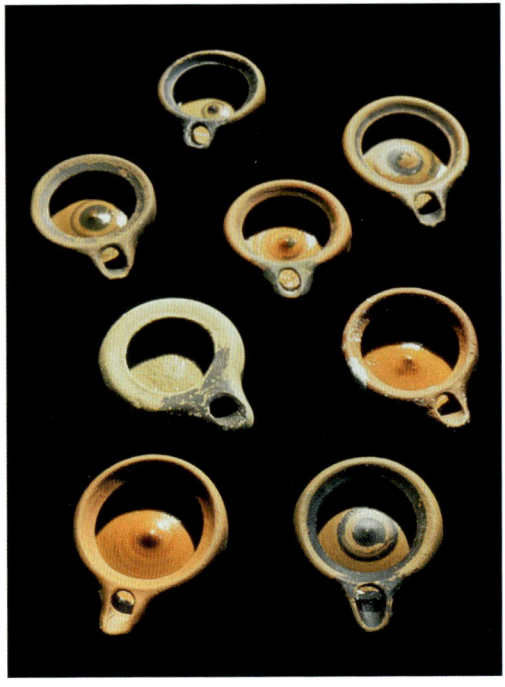

Several small lamps were found at the Tektas Burnu site.

© INA

An *askos* (decanter) in excellent condition.

© INA

cargo included smaller quantities of jars from Chios, Samos, the Troad, and the northern Aegean.

Pottery from the wreck appears to have been locally made in Ionia or on Chios and includes a modest assortment of two-handled drinking cups (*kantharoi*), one-handled bowls, table amphorae, oil lamps, a jug, a water pitcher (*hydria*), and a large wine container (*askos*). Finewares are curiously scarce, being limited to a stamped black-glaze Attic *kantharos* and two small perfume vessels: a black glaze *askos* and a lovely creamy white stone *alabastron*.

During the first summer season, archaeologists uncovered a white marble disc, approximately 14cm in diameter, at the shallowest end of the

Amphorae at the Tektas Burnu site, a photo from the 1999 excavation.

© INA

wreck site (38m down). The disc, pierced by a lead spike, still carried the remains of painted decoration on its slightly convex exterior.

The following summer, when a second identical disc was found only a metre away from the first, team members were certain that they had recovered the ship's two *ophthalmoi*, or eyes. Vase paintings illustrate how eyes were often attached to Greek ships, on each side of the bow, to protect the ship from evil and help it to 'see' its way through rough seas.

Almost nothing of the ship's hull was preserved on the rocky bottom, but for a diverse collection of lead and copper fasteners. Fourteen lead bars found scattered around the wreck represent the remains of five individual anchors. These lead bars once formed the cores of wooden anchor stocks, created by pouring molten lead into a wooden stock in order to give it

The first *ophthalmos* discovered. The *ophthalmoi* were the 'eyes' of Greek ships.

© INA

Chytrai, clay pots, found at the Tektas Burnu site.

© INA

weight. One of the lead cores still had tiny wood fragments attached to it and subsequent analyses indicated that the wood was elm. During the last weeks of the final excavation season, archaeologists located the lead remains of the fifth anchor under 1m of sand, in 55m of water, at the base of the shelf on which the wreck is situated. The location of an anchor at this depth suggests that it had been cast out in an early, but futile attempt to keep the ship from being destroyed on the treacherous, rocky coast.

At the time that this small, local merchant ship was being cast against the rocks at Tektas Burnu, Athens was the cultural epicentre of the Greek world. Ancient authors and playwrights describe the wide array of raw materials and luxury items that regularly arrived into the Athenian port-city of Piraeus. The evidence from Tektas Burnu points to the existence of regional trade networks outside Athens, supplied by small ships travelling short distances to various coastal cities. Project historian William Murray describes the Tektas Burnu ship as the ancient equivalent of a FedEx truck.

The Tektas Burnu shipwreck excavation was funded by the Institute of Nautical Archeology, Texas A&M University, the National Geographic Society, the National Endowment for the Humanities, and Turkish Airlines.

The Kyrenia wreck

This 4th century BC ship was discovered in 1967 at a depth of 30m, by Andreas Cariolou, a Cypriot diver. When Michael Katzev, an archaeologist from Yale University, was informed of the discovery, he decided to launch an excavation of the site in 1968.

The first stages were devoted to cleaning the site in order to free artefacts or other trapped items using the sediment pump, a piece of equipment vital for underwater excavation. If skilfully done, this technique helps archaeologists extricate tiny, fragile objects without causing any damage to them. The second stage consisted of compiling a site map. To do this, the divers had

Pottery jars and ancient wreckage found during the archaeological excavation of the Kyrenia wreck. Conical pottery jars displayed on fragments of hull, dating from around 300 BC.

© James Davis, Eye Ubiquitous/CORBIS

systematically to make a note of the longitude, latitude, orientation and gradient of every object found on the seabed. A grid was also put in place to finalise the site map. By this stage of the excavation, the archaeologists already had a clearer vision of their goal.

Kyrenia had been carrying 404 amphorae, most of which remained intact. Ten varieties of earthenware jars were discovered, as well as millstones and almonds. The diverse nature of the cargo illustrates the type of goods ships carried in classical times.

Next the archaeologists discovered the ship's hull, which was 14.75m long by 3.4m wide. The Mediterranean is full of ancient wrecks, but very few have their wooden framework intact. The Kyrenia ship, on the other hand, had remained in a surprisingly good condition, and is therefore considered a unique discovery. Due to the protective layer of sand covering it, two-thirds of its hull was well preserved.

Testing a model of an ancient Greek ship, a reconstruction based on the Kyrenia wreck.

© Jonathan Blair/CORBIS

The next step was to raise these invaluable finds from what had been their resting place for almost 2,000 years. The first to be extracted were the amphorae and other artefacts, which were immediately protected from the elements, cleaned, and plunged into desalination tanks. The researchers hoped then to raise the entire ship, though its remnants no longer held together in one piece. The wood's mass was almost 75% water after lying on the seabed for so long. It was therefore impossible to raise it without damage to its structure. The archaeologists decided to dismantle the ribs of the ship using a pneumatic saw, and strip the planking from the hull. It was methodically dried, then injected with a chemical conservation resin, designed by Francis Talbot-Vasiliadou.

An eclectic cargo

The majority of the 404 amphorae were manufactured in Rhodes in the 4th century BC as containers for wine. At that time, Rhodian wine was widely consumed across the Greek world. Other amphorae, some bearing stamps on the handles, came from Samos and Cyprus. Thirty-four were marked with the letters 'API', almost certainly the initials of the manufacturer. The other eight types of jar were much more sparsely represented. They must have contained provisions for the crew, or unusual goods.

The cargo also contained thousands of almonds, found heaped up in different parts of the ship, and 29 millstones arranged beneath the lower row of amphorae, possibly acting as ballast. Seven bronze coins were found and analysed, one of which had on one side a shield decorated with a lion's head, and on the other, a Macedonian helmet. It had been minted during the reign of Antigonos Monophthalmos, 'the One-Eyed', between 316 and 310 BC. Another coin had a helmet on one side, and a ship's prow on the other. It dated from the reign of Demetrios Poliorkitis, 'the Besieger', son of Antigonos, between 306 and 294 BC.

The contents of the cargo suggested a possible itinerary for the ship. It had crossed the Aegean Sea and stopped in several of the Dodecanese islands. The amphorae came from Rhodes, the millstones from Nissyros, and the almonds from Cyprus.

Other finds provided clues to the everyday life of the crew: small pieces of pottery found fore and aft of the main cargo indicated that there were two separate compartments. Cups were found at the bow end, showing that drinking water had been stored there. Kitchen utensils and crockery were found aft: black varnished plates, bowls, wooden spoons, cups, saltcellars, and oil jugs. There were four of each kind of these utensils, so it can be assumed that there were at least four sailors on board when the ship wrecked. On the other hand, no stove or cooking equipment was found, which led the archaeologists to suggest that the crew would eat on dry land, having lit a fire on the beach. The team of archaeologists recovered sinkers used on fishing lines – the sailors must therefore have fished by day. Only one piece of a terracotta lamp was found. It seemed then that the boat did not sail by night.

The ship's construction

The ship was built according to principles quite typical of the era – the 'shell-first' method. Its external planking was built starting with the hull, then came the framework, assembled using copper tacks. This had a lead sheathing, fixed with copper nails, intended to protect the wood from sea worms. The Greeks used this protective system from the 5th century BC. Lead sheets and carpenters' mallets

The architect and sailor Richard Steffy inspects the hull of the Kyrenia.

© Jonathan Blair/CORBIS

II. Thalassa, the Greek sea

Reconstructing the Kyrenia ship.
© Jonathan Blair/CORBIS

found on the wreck would have been used for repairing this sheathing when necessary.

Near to the stem post, in a section which has not survived, divers found a mast step. This mast being near to the prow, it is likely for reasons of balance that there would have been a second mast affixed aft. The sail did not therefore cross the boat's width, but would instead have been positioned lengthways and its dimensions have been estimated at 64m². Before the discovery of the ship at Kyrenia, it was believed that this type of rigging only dated back to the 2nd century BC, whereas the carbon 14 analysis made of the ship's wood proved it had been built around 388 BC, ±44 years. This rigging method then was invented as early as the 4th century BC.

Was the shipwreck the result of old age or a pirate attack?

The archaeological team first ascribed the shipwreck to the poor state of the ship. A carbon 14 analysis of the almonds indicated that they had been harvested in 288 BC, taking into account a margin of error of 62 years.

The ship may therefore have been almost 100 years old when it sank, and must also have undergone a number of repairs, as the state of the framework attests. Stormy seas may then have been enough to break the ship in two.

But archaeologists revised their theories upon further investigation. They discovered iron spears under the hull, and others stuck into the side of the boat, indicating that pirates must have attacked the ship. At the time, the coastline of Kyrenia was scattered with small creeks, scarcely visible from the ship. Pirates hid their boats there, raiding merchant ships to pillage the cargo and capture their crews.

This could explain the disappearance of the crew members and their possessions. The pirates would have taken the men to sell them at slave markets, removing any valuables from the ship. They probably scuttled the ship by cutting holes in its sides – hence the spears found around the wreck – thereby disposing of the evidence of their crime.

A unique find

The Kyrenia wreck was such a remarkable discovery that the archaeologists planned in 1982 to build a replica of the ship. The project was undertaken by Michael Katzev and the INA (of which he is a founder), with the HIPNT (Hellenic Institute for the Preservation of Nautical Tradition) team, under the direction of Harry Tzallas and Professor J. Richard Steffy, a member of the archaeological department of UNESCO.

They planned to build an exact replica capable of navigating Greek seas, identical to the original and built using contemporary construction methods. This ambitious idea required three years of labour before the replica, named Kyrenia II, became a reality. The greatest difficulty was the shipbuilding method, which had not been employed for centuries. Fortunately, the archaeological excavations of the site had given enough accurate results to facilitate its reconstruction. The team meticulously replicated the methods used two millennia previously. From the nails to the wood, the tools to the painting, the hull to the mast – everything was copied exactly from the original. Following ancient Greek tradition, two blue eyes surveying the seas were painted on each side of the boat.

Kyrenia II was launched on 22 June 1985. In September 1986, she set sail from Mikrolimano at Piraeus, for Paphos, Cyprus, covering a distance of 827km in less than a month. The speed and capabilities of the ship are exceptional. Other projects are now underway for this ship. Kyrenia II may be used to transport copper from Cyprus to Greece for the 2004 Olympic Games in Athens, to symbolise Cyprus's contribution to the event.

The Antikythera wreck

At the end of the 1st century BC, a merchant ship sank off the island of Antikythera, in southern Greece.

Almost two thousand years later it was spotted by sponge fishermen, and in 1900 the Greek government was prompted to launch one of the first underwater archaeological campaigns. The cargo proved to be extraordinarily rich, making the mission a real success. One object in particular was astounding. It was made up of metal cogs, and lay hidden among other finds.

In the summer of 1900, Captain Kondos, in charge of a sponge-fishing ship, had one of his divers return to the ship in a state of panic. Elias Stadiados swore that he had seen a pile of naked women's corpses on the seabed. Captain Kondos quickly realised that these were in fact ancient statues, since he was familiar with the stories sponge fishermen often told each other of treasure lying at the bottom of the sea.

When the wreck was found, Kondos did not immediately inform the authorities. It was common for cargoes to be pillaged and anything of worth to be resold. At Simi, the divers' small home village, gossip began to spread about the sale of several small bronze statuettes in Alexandria.

Kondos decided to alert the government, which agreed to use his boat and divers to help with the excavation.

The early days of underwater archaeology

The Greek government understood, over a century ago, the incredible potential of the then unnamed field of underwater archaeology. Unfortunately, the techniques and equipment at the excavators' disposal were rudimentary.

No survey was done, and no photography or plan made before the objects were raised. Nor were any steps taken to prevent the objects' exposure to the open air. Many objects were therefore lost before they could be studied by archaeologists, but luckily the remainder was enough to gain an impression of the cargo. Bronze and marble statues, jewels, coins, earthenware jars and crockery could be examined in great detail.

All the artefacts were taken to the Greek National Museum. The divers had worked in extremely difficult conditions, their lives constantly at risk. Two were paralysed, another died. When winter and bad weather came, the team was ready to leave, delighted with their discoveries in spite of the hardships, and exhausted from all the work. They had also found tiny fragments of wood, which were certain to have come from the ship's hull.

However, not until Captain Jacques-Yves Cousteau arrived with his team in 1953, was the hull found. Using more modern equipment, divers located it buried under 40cm of sand.

Cousteau and his team launched a second excavation of the site in 1976, during which they discovered Pergamon coins dating from between 88 and 86 BC.

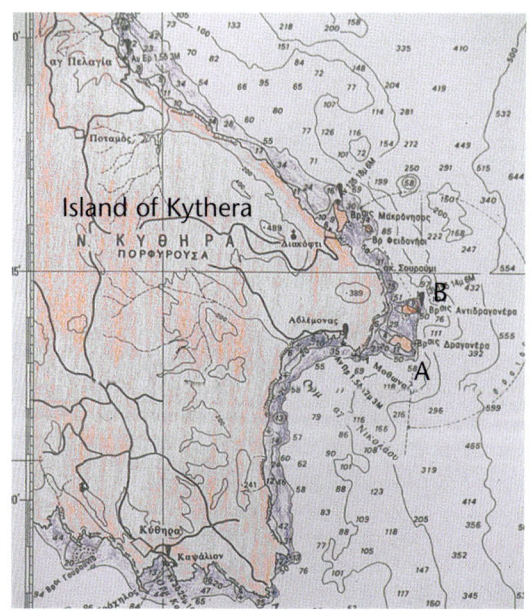

A map of the island of Kythera, showing the islets of Dragonera (A) and Antidragonera (B), site of a 4th century BC wreck. Antikythera lies 38km to the southeast.

© HIMA

The Antidragonera wreck

Dimitris Kourkoumelis

In 1993, HIMA, directed by myself, embarked upon underwater research off the island of Kythera in southern Greece.

During this research, nine pyramidal stone anchors were found north of Antidragonera, an islet off the southeast coast of Kythera. These were similar to some found in Passalimani port, Piraeus, and on the wrecks Madonnina and Ognina 4.

The Antidragonera excavation, part of HIMA's research programme, lasted from 1994 to 2000.

The anchors, found in a little bay on the north side of Antidragonera, fall into two groups. The first four are smaller, and were discovered on the bay's seabed, at a depth of 9m. They were probably used by the sailors to stabilise the ship in the bay, to protect themselves from bad weather.

The five anchors in the second group were larger, and were found 150m nearer the northeastern cape of the Antidragonera islet. Four of these have been raised to the surface. Their excavation, along with the discovery of some ceramics, seemed to suggest that this is the most likely location for

The pyramid-shaped stone anchors.

© HIMA

where the shipwreck took place. The ceramics discovered during the excavation do not appear to be part of the ship's main cargo, which was made up largely of everyday objects, such as plates, lamps, *lekanides*, pitchers, mortars, bowls and similar objects, amphorae for transporting goods, and a large *pithos*.

Some lead objects were also found, probably belonging to the deadwork (upper sections of the ship), and at least three bronze nails, possibly from the ship's hull. All these objects excavated from the site mean we can date it to the end of the 4th century BC.

The studies made of the wreck, and the publication of material from the studies, are ongoing, but certain conclusions can already be drawn. There is a striking resemblance between this wreck at Antidragonera, and the Madonnina and Ognina 4 wrecks. The few transport amphorae and *pithoi* are not the usual cargo of a merchant ship, and the ceramics found aboard could not have been there for commercial reasons.

It is therefore likely that these ships, if used for trading, transported perishable goods such as wheat.

One theory advanced by researchers is that the three anchors found on each of the three wrecks, which seem to be Archaic, were used by military vessels. However, this theory cannot be proven, since at the time sailors used stock anchors.

Finally, it is worth noting that the three wrecks date from the same period, the second half of the 4th century BC.

Ceramics and bronze nails from the Antidragonera wreck.

© HIMA

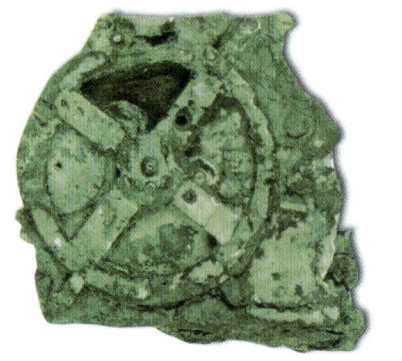

The largest remaining components of the Antikythera mechanism. From these humble fragments, great theories have been born.

© National Archaeological Museum, Athens

A mysterious device

It was some time before researchers studying the Antikythera wreck noticed the four fragments of a strange object, lying in a wooden box. They were brought to Athens and stored in the museum vaults before anybody showed any interest in them. At first it was believed that they were part of an *astrolabe*, an ancient navigation instrument. Experts refuted this theory, however. Even if the Greeks were technically capable of manufacturing such an object, the instrument in question could certainly not be an example of one.

In 1951, a scientific historian from Yale University, Derek de Solla Price, began to study the device – a project which would occupy him until 1974. Preliminary work on the bronze fragments revealed that the device had consisted of dials set into a wooden box, which contained numerous cogs. The box was covered with inscriptions, including a calendar of the stars.

But the most significant discovery was that the mechanism included a system of differential gears. Price was amazed at this as, until this point, historians believed that the earliest example of such an advanced mechanism was a clock built in 1575. For over a decade, Price struggled to reconstruct the mechanism from the corroded fragments.

In 1971, Price analysed the bronze object using x-ray, revealing the gadget's original arrangement and enabling him to reconstruct it. He obtained a composition of at least 30 cogwheels whose simultaneous movement tracked the movement of the sun and the moon, in relation to the constellations of the zodiac. Although later analysis suggested that the mechanism was even more developed than Price had thought, he was nonetheless proved correct in his supposition of the complex technical capabilities of the ancient Greeks.

Michael Wright, curator of mechanical engineering at the Science Museum, London, went on to study the device using linear tomography. Wright, with the collaboration of Allan Bromley, a computer science professor at the University of Sydney, uncovered the exact position of each cog, contradicting certain elements of Price's hypothesis. Wright considered that Price had not been precise enough in his studies, drawing conclusions too quickly. Of course, since so few fragments of the mechanism survive, any scientific conclusion is difficult and risks inaccuracies.

Wright identified a previously unnoticed feature at the centre of the large wheel that turns once in a year with the sun, and proposed that this held a fixed central wheel, around which other cogs, all now lost, rotated in an epicyclic motion.

Most Greek astronomers believed that the sun, moon and other planets moved around the earth. However, a simple circular motion could not reproduce the observed changes in speed with which the bodies seemed to move across the sky, although an epicyclic system could. Wright asserted that the instrument could have been designed to demonstrate this epicyclical theory. In fact, what survives could have been the basis of three motions: the solar theory of Hipparchus, and the simple epicyclic theory of the two 'inferior' planets, Mercury and Venus.

Wright also pointed out that someone capable of designing such a sophisticated device may well have wanted to include other astronomical phenomena, most obviously Hipparchus's lunar theory and the simple epicyclic theory of the 'superior' planets Mars, Jupiter and Saturn. Wright showed that these features could be added consistently with the original fragments, to turn the display into a complete planetarium, and he has constructed a model to demonstrate this theory.

In Wright's reconstruction of the front dial of the mechanism, seven separate bronze pointers move over a circular dial to show the positions of the sun, moon and other planets in the zodiac, on any given day, indicated by an eighth hand. Wright demonstrates that these positions can be indicated with astonishing long-term accuracy, although the simple epicyclic theory, the best planetary theory available when the instrument was made, leads to short-term fluctuations.

Ancient writers, most notably Cicero – a contemporary of the shipwreck – refer to devices showing the motions of the sun, moon and five planets, but scholars have been uncertain how literally to interpret their statements. Wright hopes that his reconstruction will demonstrate the complexity of the mechanism and the reliability of these ancient accounts. He is now working on a more complete reconstruction of the whole instrument.

No hypothesis can be entirely proven, given the lack of evidence; a few small fragments are all that is left. However, modern technology has already given us an important insight into this extraordinary mechanism, so it can only be hoped that we will be able to glean more information in the future, or that other mechanisms from the same era will be found.

Bronze statue from the Antikythera wreck.
© National Archaeological Museum, Athens

Made in Rhodes?

The context in which the device was found helped Price to estimate the date of the object's construction: 87 BC. But who in Greece could have been capable of building such a complex mechanism?

The amphorae in the cargo came from Rhodes. Furthermore, at the time, Rhodes was considered to be one of the most scientifically and intellectually advanced centres in the ancient world. Its navy was, and remained, one of the most formidable in ancient times, until the Romans rose to prominence 40 years later.

Other artefacts from the site proved the ship's point of origin was modern day Turkey. But this was not necessarily the origin of the instrument – indeed the mass of evidence shows that it could have come from anywhere in the ancient Greek world.

From the discoveries of a sponge fisherman, underwater archaeology has revealed highly advanced ancient navigation techniques, opening new doors on the history of these ancient peoples. If the Greeks could build a device of such precision and complexity, it is possible that other objects or creations of this type are lying underwater, waiting to be discovered.

Conclusion

The Romans built over many ancient monuments in eastern and western Phoenicia, transforming them beyond recognition. As a result there have been few artefacts dug up on land that provide evidence of the Phoenicians' great genius. Underwater archaeology has therefore played a vital role in furthering our knowledge of this mysterious people.

It is appropriate that so much of what we know about the Phoenicians has been garnered from the sea, since they were particularly renowned for their harbours and seafaring. The ports at Tyre, Sidon and the *cothon* at Motya remind us of the Phoenicians' ingenuity and remarkably advanced engineering. Greek and Roman shipwrights owed a huge debt to the Phoenicians.

Greek civilisation is much better documented through ancient texts, and archaeological excavations on land have also provided ample evidence of the inspired architectural and artistic evolution of the Hellenic peoples. However, underwater archaeological research has challenged many previously accepted theories of Aegean economic history. The conclusions drawn from the Tektas Burnu excavations are a good example of this.

Equally, the discovery of cargoes of ceramics and amphorae has filled in the gaps in our knowledge of Greek arts and crafts, from the Minoan Period to the end of the Classical Age, through the Mycenaean and Archaic eras.

A great number of Mediterranean sites remain to be explored, and happily for archaeologists, historians and all those interested in Antiquity, they will undoubtedly provide fresh clues to the Greek and Phoenician civilisations.

Glossary

Achaeans: Indo-European people from the Danubian region and the southern Russian steppes. They invaded mainland Greece towards the end of the Bronze Age, circa 1900 BC.

Aeolus: god of the winds in Greek mythology.

Alexander the Great (356-323 BC): son of Olympias, princess of Epirus, and of Philip II, King of Macedonia. Alexander III the Great received a princely education, mastered the art of war and was tutored by Aristotle. He became King of Macedonia (336-323 BC) and continued his father's expansionist policy by establishing an empire. He is renowned for becoming ruler of Greece, Egypt and Asia. His exploits are recorded in the Bible and the Koran, and have made him a legendary hero, still a popular figure today, well beyond the lands he once controlled.

Antigonos Monophthalmos (381-301 BC): known as 'the One-Eyed', Alexander the Great's lieutenant and successor in Macedonia attempted to continue his predecessor's expansionist policy, but was defeated and killed at Ipsos in 301 BC.

Apollonius (262-190 BC): Greek mathematician and astronomer.

apotropaic: adjective from the Greek *apotropaios*, meaning 'which is intended to avert evil influence'.

Aramaeans: Semitic peoples from Northern Mesopotamia, said to have come from Aram (or ancient Syria). They founded various states in Syria and Lebanon in the 13th century BC. In the 8th century BC, their language became the universal language for the ancient Near East until the Arab conquest in the 7th century AD.

Archimedes (c. 287-212 BC): Greek physicist, mathematician and engineer. His numerous and impressive inventions made him the most famous scientist of Antiquity.

Aristotle (384-322 BC): known as 'the Stagirite', disciple of Plato, tutor to Alexander the Great, this Greek philosopher founded the Lyceum, or Peripatetic schools, and wrote numerous treatises dealing with every aspect of contemporary knowledge.

Arrian: Greek historian and philosopher, disciple of Epictetus.

Artemis: Greek goddess of hunting and the moon (Diana is her Roman equivalent), daughter of Zeus and Leto and Apollo's twin sister.

askoi (sing. *askos*): shallow flasks with a spout at one end and a handle across the top.

Baal Hammon: divinity worshipped by various western Semitic peoples, including the Canaanites. Baal Hammon was particularly associated with the atmospheric phenomena on which harvests depended.

bireme: ancient galley with two banks of oars.

Bronze Age: period which saw the spread of metallurgy in the ancient world. It is divided into the early (2500-1600 BC), middle (1600-1300 BC) and late (1300-900 BC) Bronze Age.

Calypso: nymph from Greek mythology and queen of the island of Ogygia. In *The Odyssey*, she takes in the shipwrecked Ulysses and he stays for 10 years.

Canaanites: Semitic peoples who invaded Syria and Palestine during the 3rd millennium BC. They settled in the coastal area and became known as the Phoenicians.

Charybdis: whirlpool in the Straits of Messina near the Scylla rock.

chôma: any pile of earth, but particularly that forming a jetty or breakwater.

chytra (pl. *chytrai*): clay vase, earthenware pot, cooking-pot.

Cicero: great Roman politician and orator (106-43 BC), famous primarily for his political speeches and philosophical treatises.

Cimon (510-449 BC): Athenian strategist, leader of the Aristocratic party, son of Miltiades. He fought successfully against the Persians and founded the first Athenian Confederacy.

Claudius Ptolemy: Greek scholar of the Alexandrian school. Known mainly in the fields of geography and astronomy.

cothon: large enclosed basin dug behind the coastline and connected to the sea by a channel.

Cronus (or Kronos): A Titan, son of Uranus (Sky) and Gaea (Earth), father of Zeus. He is the father of the first generation of Hellenic gods, the Titans.

Cyclades (or Kuklades): archipelago of Greek islands in the Aegean Sea, so called because it forms a circle around Delos.

Cyrenaica: North African region on the Mediterranean coast between Egypt and Greater Syria. The Greeks founded colonies here including Cyrene.

deigma **(pl.** *deigmata***):** 'which proves itself', i.e. evidence.

Dimitrios Poliorkitis: son of Antigonos Monophthalmos, 'the Beseiger'.

Ephesus: Greek city of Ionia, founded in the 10th century BC. One of the great trading centres on the coast of Asia Minor.

Euxine Sea: ancient name of the Black Sea, said to be dangerous because of its storms and the inhabitants of its shores. Calling it the 'hospitable sea' was a way of warding off misfortune.

Ezekiel (627-570 BC): third of the four main prophets in the Bible. He foretold the capture of Jerusalem by Nebuchadnezzar as well as Israel's rebirth.

gamma rays: high-energy electromagnetic radiation. The rays are emitted when radioactive substances decay.

gaulos: originally referring to a rounded vase or basket, the word came to signify the round-shaped Phoenician merchant ships.

Greater Greece: all the colonies founded by the Greeks in Southern Italy and Sicily from the 8th century BC onwards.

grid layout: marking out the excavation site using a network of taut cables crossing each other at right angles. Each find can then be given a grid reference, enabling archaeologists to plot them accurately on the map.

Hades: Greek god of the underworld (Pluto was the Roman equivalent).

Heracles: Greek hero of superhuman strength, son of Zeus and Alceme (Hercules was the Roman equivalent).

Herodotus (484-420 BC): Greek historian, known as the 'Father of History'. A friend of Sophocles and Pericles in Athens, this great traveller was the author of several works, including *The History*, a major source of information for students of the Median Wars and Greek civilisation.

Hesiod (mid-8th century BC): Greek poet and author of *The Theogony*, regarded at the time as Homer's equal. His writings contain invaluable information about the Archaic era.

Hipparchus: tyrant of Athens from 527 to 514 BC.

Hiram I: King of Tyre circa 969-935 BC. He supplied Solomon with artists and materials to build the temple in Jerusalem, and with seafarers for expeditions.

Homer: the most famous Greek poet, known particularly for his two epics *The Iliad* and *The Odyssey*. His existence appeared to be substantiated in Antiquity but is disputed by some modern scholars.

hydria: large Greek three-handled pitcher, one of which was vertical.

The Iliad: Homer's epic in 24 cantos, including an account of an episode during the Trojan War.

Ionians: the peoples who occupied Ionia, the central part of the coastal region of Asia Minor, populated by Greeks from Europe following the Dorian invasions.

Iron Age: period following the Stone Age or the Bronze Age, depending on the continent. Its name refers to the spread of iron metallurgy.

kados (pl. *kadoi*): vase, pitcher or jar.

kantharos (pl. *kantharoi*): two-handled drinking cup.

krater: large vase or large wide-mouthed, two-handled bowl used by the Ancients for mixing wine with water.

linear tomography: a procedure normally used in medicine. This technique provides images of successive plane sections of a specific object or organ using x-rays or ultrasound.

Mardonios (died in 479 BC): son-in-law of Darius I. This Persian general was entrusted by Darius with the subjugation of Greece in 492 BC. He failed, but nevertheless became commander-in-chief of the Persian army in 480 BC and occupied Boetia and Attica. He was killed at the battle of Plataea, where his army was defeated by the Persians

Melos (or Milos): an island in the Cyclades.

Minos: legendary king of Crete, son of Zeus and Europa. He forced the Athenians to send seven boys and seven girls each year to be fed to the Minotaur. After his death, he became one of the three judges of the underworld.

mortise: a rectangular recess cut in a piece of wood to receive a projection or 'tenon' on another piece and thereby form a 'mortise and tenon' joint.

Nebuchadnezzar II: King of Babylon (605-562 BC), which he made the capital of the Eastern world.

Nectanebo I: Egyptian monarch, founder of the 30th (and final) Dynasty. He died in 360 BC.

Neith: divinity from the ancient Egyptian city of Sais on the Nile delta.

neosoikoi: ship sheds (from *neos*, new, and *oikos*, building).

nesef: Syrian coin weighing 10.3g.

Notos: personification of the word *notos*, meaning 'southerly wind'.

The Odyssey: epic poem in 24 cantos recounting the adventures of Ulysses after the taking of Troy.

oenochoe: vessel used for ladling wine from a bowl into a cup.

ophthalmos (pl. *opthalmoi*): meaning 'eye'.

penteconter: ship with 50 oars.

Pericles (495-429 BC): Athenian statesman whose part in Athens's political and cultural development was such that the most brilliant century in the history of classical Greece became known as 'the Century of Pericles'.

Philip II of Macedonia (382-336 BC): became regent and then king of Macedonia from 359 to 336 BC. Defeated the coalition of Athens and Thebes at the battle of Chaeronea in 338 BC. Father of Alexander the Great.

photogrammetry: the application of stereophotography in surveying and mapping.

photomosaic: a composite photograph created by placing together several separate photographs of approximately the same scale.

pithos (pl. *pithoi*): barrel or jug for wine.

Pliny the Elder (23-79 AD): Roman soldier and politician who, in his retirement, wrote *Natural History*. This vast work remained the authoritative scientific reference encyclopaedia until the Middle Ages.

Plutarch (c. 46-120 AD): moralist, philosopher and historian who wrote *Parallel Lives*, a series of biographies (of Alexander, Caesar and Antony) in Greek, as well as other works which provide historians and archaeologists with a large amount of information.

polis: Greek word meaning 'town', but also meaning a system of political organisation.

polychromy: the art of painting or decorating in several colours.

Polycrates: tyrant of Samos from 533 to 522 BC. He led his city to a period of great prosperity.

Poseidon: Greek god of the sea. Son of Cronus and Rhea, and brother of Zeus and Hades.

prophylaxis: all precautionary measures intended to prevent the spread of one or more diseases.

protome: a piece of sculpture representing the bust of a human or the forepart of an animal.

pyxis (pl. *pyxides*): box for medicines and perfumes in a variety of shapes.

qedet (or *kite*): Egyptian coin weighing between 9.1g and 9.3g. Ten *qedets* made a *deben*, 10 *debens* made a *sep*.

ROV (Remotely operated vehicle): robots operated from the surface to carry out underwater tasks impossible for humans.

Scylla: rock in the Straits of Messina opposite Charybdis.

sediment extractor: instrument used in underwater excavation, which operates through the Venturi effect caused by the high-pressure injection of water into a nozzle. It allows the user to control the material being extracted with great precision.

sidescan sonar: sensor giving an acoustic image of the ocean floor within a band of 50m-150m on either side of the ship. Processing the sonar data produces a mosaic of the surveyed area by juxtaposing geographically positioned bands.

skyphos (pl. *skyphoi*): a tall stemless drinking cup or vase.

Solomon: son of David and Bathsheba. He was the third King of the Hebrews.

stem: the entire forepart of a vessel's keel.

stoa: portico, covered colonnade.

Strabo (66 BC-24 AD): Greek geographer from Amaseia (now Amasya). A great traveller who wrote *Geography*, providing many details about this period in history.

Sulla (138-78 BC): Roman statesman and general.

Telemachus: hero of Greek mythology. Son of Ulysses and Penelope.

temenos: sacred enclosure of a temple in ancient Greece.

tenon: a projection on the end of a piece of wood made to fit into a cavity or 'mortise' to form a mortise and tenon joint.

thalassocracy: nation with mastery of the sea.

Themistocles (528-462 BC): Athenian statesman and general. He made Athens into a major maritime power by reorganizing its fleet and developing Piraeus.

Theseus: hero of Greek mythology, celebrated for killing the Minotaur, thereby freeing Athens from Minos. He became king of Athens and established its first institutions.

Thucydides: Greek historian and author of the *History of the Peloponnesian War*.

tophet: Carthaginian burial urn filled with the ashes of children sacrificed to Baal Hammon or Baal-Moloch, or the place of the same name, dedicated to the god Baal and goddess Tanit, where child sacrifices are said to have taken place between 715 and 146 BC.

trireme: ancient Greek warship with three superposed banks of oars.

Ulysses: hero of Greek mythology whose exploits are recounted by Homer. King of Ithaca, husband of Penelope and father of Telemachus.

Virgil (70-19 BC): Latin poet and author of many famous works.

Xenophon (430-355 BC): Greek philosopher, writer and politician. He was a disciple of Socrates.

zephyr: soft, gentle wind.

Zeus: king of the gods. God of light and lightning, ruler of the celestial realm. Son of Kronos and Rhea.

Bibliography

Ballard R. D., "Ashkelon", *National Geographic Magazine*, vol. 199, No. 1, 2001.

Ballard R. D. et al., "Iron Age shipwrecks in deep water off Ashkelon, Israel", *American Journal of Archeology*, vol. 106, No. 2, 2002.

Blackman D. J., "The ship-sheds", in Morrison J. S. and Williams R.T., *Greek Oared Ships 900-322 BC*, Cambridge University Press, 1968.

Empereur J.-Y., Archonidou A. (1987), then Simossi A. (1988-1993), *Chroniques du BCH* de 1987 à 1993.

Frost F. J., "The 'Harbour' at Halieis", Avner Raban ed., *Harbour Archaeology*, British Archaeological Reports, Oxford, 1985.

Garland R., *The Piraeus*, Bristol Classical Press, 2001.

Jameson M. H., "Excavations at Porto Cheli and vicinity, preliminary report, I: Halieis, 1962-1968", *Hesperia 38*, 1968.

Jameson M. H., "Excavations at Porto Cheli", *Archaiologikon Deltion 26*, 1971.

Jameson M. H., "The excavation of a drowned Greek temple", *Scientific American 231*, 1974.

Jameson M. H., "The submerged sanctuary of Apollo at Halieis in the Argolid of Greece", *National Geographic Society Research Reports*, 1982.

Kahanov Y., "Conflicting evidence for defining the origin of the Ma'agan Mikhael shipwreck", Tzalas H. ed., *Tropis IV*, 1996.

Kahanov Y., "Wood conservation of the Ma'agan Mikhael shipwreck", *International Journal of Nautical Archaeology 26*, 1997.

Kahanov Y., "The Ma'agan Mikhael ship (Israel): a comparative study of its hull construction", *Archaeonautica 14*, éditions CNRS, 1999.

Karageorghis V., Lolos Y. G., Vichos Y. et al., *The Point Iria Wreck: a guide to the exhibition of the wrecked cargo in the Museum of Spetses*, Hellenic Institute of Marine Archaeology, Athens, 1998 (in Greek).

Kourkoumelis D., "The Antidragonera wreck (Kythera, end of 4th century BC)", *Archäologie unter Wasser 3*, Bayerische Gesellschaft für Unterwasserarchäologie, 1998.

Kourkoumelis D., "Les ancres pyramidales en pierre et les techniques d'ancrage: le cas de l'épave d'Antidragonera (Cythère, IVe siècle av. J.-C.)", Brun J.-P., Jockey P. ed., *Techniques et sociétés en Méditerranée: hommage à Marie-Claire Amouretti*, Maison méditerranéenne des sciences de l'homme, Travaux du Centre Camille Jullian, Maisonneuve et Larose, 2001.

Kourkoumelis D., "Underwater excavation at the Antidragonera shipwreck of Kythera, the 1997 and 2000 campaigns", *Enalia*, vol. VI, 2002.

Linder E., "Ma'agan Micha'el shipwreck: excavating an ancient merchantman", *Biblical Archaeology Review 18*, 1992.

Linder E. and Rosloff, J., "The Ma'agan Mikhael shipwreck", Tzalas H. ed., *Tropis III*, Hellenic Institute for the Preservation of Nautical Tradition, 1995.

Lolos Y. G., "Late Cypro-Mycenaean seafaring: new evidence from sites in the Saronic and the Argolic Gulfs", Karageorghis V., Michaelides D. ed., *Proceedings of the International Symposium: Cyprus and the Sea*, 1995.

Lolos Y. G., "Commercial stirrup jars and Mediterranean sea routes in the Late Bronze Age: the underwater evidence", *Le rotte nell' antico Mediterraneo: Proggeti di ricerca nell' ambito dei Beni archeologici sommersi*, Italy, due to be published 2003.

Lovén B., *The Zea Shipsheds – the buildings' utility in reconstructing the Athenian Trireme*, Tzalas H. ed., 2002.

Mattingly H., "Find from Piraeus", N. Chr., Vol. VII, 1927.

Morrison J. S., Coates J. F., Rankov N. B., *The Athenian Trireme, The History and Reconstruction of an Ancient Greek Warship*, Cambridge University Press, 2nd edition 2000.

Phelps W. and Lolos Y., *The Point Iria Wreck: Interconnections in the Mediterranean circa 1200 BC,* Y. Vichos ed., Hellenic Institute of Marine Archaeology, Athens, 1999.

Powell A., "Archaeology team helps find oldest deep-sea shipwrecks", *Harvard Gazette*, 16 September 1999.

Stager L. E., "Ashkelon and the archaeology of destruction", *Biblical Archaeology Review*, 1996.

Rice R., "The Antikythera mechanism: physical and intellectual salvage from the 1st century BC", USNA Eleventh Naval History Symposium, 1995.

Rosloff J., "A one-armed anchor of c. 400 BC from the Ma'agan Michael vessel, Israel", *International Journal of Nautical Archaeology*, 1991.

Schloen D., "Recent discoveries at Ashkelon", The Oriental Institute Notes and News 145, 1995.

Steinhauer G.A., "La découverte de l'arsenal du Philon", *Tropis IV*, Athens, 1996.

Touchais G., "Chronique des fouilles en 1978 – le Pirée", BCH 103, 1979.

Vichos Y., Tsouchlos N., Papathanassopoulos G. "Thalassa: L'Égée préhistorique et la mer", *Aegaeum 7*, Liege, 1991.

Vichos Y. and Lolos Y., "The Cypro-Mycenaean wreck at Point Iria in the Argolic Gulf: first thoughts on the origin and the nature of the vessel", Swiny S., Hohlfelder R. L., Wylde Swiny H. eds, *Res Maritimae, Cyprus and the Eastern Mediterranean from Prehistory to Late Antiquity,* Scholars Press, Atlanta, Georgia, 1997.

Von Eickstedt K. V., *Beiträge zur Topographie des antiken Piräus*, Athens, 1991.

Wright M., "A new spin on the world's oldest cogwheels", Science Museum Press Office, London, 2002.

Wright M., "A clockwork computer: the Antikythera mechanism", *The Economist,* London, 21 September 2002.